•Bartholomew

WALK
NORTHUMBRIA

by Richard Hallewell
Illustrations by Rebecca Johnstone

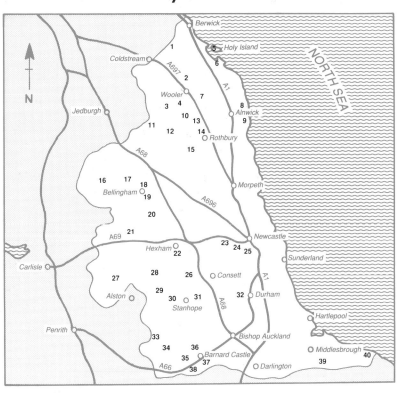

Bartholomew
A Division of HarperCollinsPublishers

Published by Bartholomew, a Division of HarperCollins*Publishers*,
12 Duncan Street, Edinburgh EH9 1TA.

A catalogue record for this book is available from the British
Library.

First published 1990
Reprinted with changes 1991

© Bartholomew 1990, 1991

Printed in Great Britain by Bartholomew,
HarperCollins*Manufacturing*, Edinburgh.

ISBN 0 7028 0959 4

Britain's landscape is changing all the time. While every care has
been taken in the preparation of this guide, Bartholomew accepts
no responsibility whatsoever for any loss, damage, injury or
inconvenience sustained or caused as a result of using this guide.

About this book

This is a book of walks, all of which can be completed within one day. They pass through every type of scenery to be found in the area - hill, farm, coastal, industrial and woodland - and vary in difficulty from gentle strolls to strenuous hill climbs. Each route is graded according to its level of difficulty, and wherever specialist hill-walking equipment is required this is specified. There is a description of each route, including information on the character and condition of the paths and a brief description of the major points of interest along the way. In addition, there is a sketch map of the route to aid navigation. Car parks, where available, are indicated on the route maps; where parking is not mentioned it may be assumed that it presents no difficulties. The availability of public conveniences and public transport on particular routes is listed on the contents page, and at the head of each route. The suitability or otherwise of the route for dogs is also indicated on the contents page. The location of each route within Northumbria is shown on the area map inside the cover of the book, and a brief description of how to reach the walk from the nearest town is provided at the start of each walk. In addition, National Grid References are provided on the maps. The use of a detailed map, in addition to this book, is advised on all A grade walks.

The following introduction provides a brief summary of the geography, history and natural history of Northumbria. Hopefully, an appreciation of the area's landscape and links with the past will add to the interest of the walks.

Before setting out, all walkers are asked to read through the section of Advice to Walkers at the end of this introduction. In the long term it never pays to become lax in taking safety precautions.

This is by no means an exhaustive list of the many fine walks in Northumbria, but it provides a core of varied, accepted routes. I hope you will find it an interesting selection.

Key

●●●	Route	Marshland	**1 foot = 0.3m**
═══	Metalled Road	······ Moorland	**1 mile = 1.6km**
++++	Railway	▲▲ Coniferous Woodland	
Ⓟ	Parking	♦♦ Broad-leaved Woodland	
🌀	Contour: shaded area is above height indicated	*i* Information Centre	

The Area

(Figures in italics refer to individual walks)

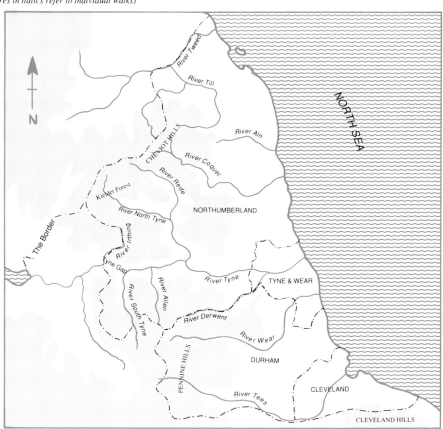

The map above shows the boundaries and main features of the area covered by this book (the map inside the front cover shows the whereabouts of the individual routes). Those who know Northumbria will already appreciate the scale and quality of the landscape of this largely unspoilt region. For those who do not, the following introduction briefly describes its major features, and outlines the history of this fascinating corner of England.

Those with an interest in Anglo-Saxon history may consider the title of this book a little misleading. The ancient kingdom of Northumbria assumed many shapes and sizes during its 350 year existence (between 604, when it was created by

Ethelfrid, and 954, when King Edred incorporated it into England), but its core is generally defined as being between the Rivers Forth and Humber: an area more than twice the size of that delineated on the map above.

The 'Northumbria' shown here, and used as the geographical basis for this book, is contained within the regional boundaries of Northumberland, Durham, Cleveland and Tyne and Wear – that is, the old (pre-1974) counties of Northumberland and Durham, plus a little of the North Riding of Yorkshire (the land south of the River Tees).

Within these boundaries is a landscape of considerable variety. Along the long North Sea coast, there are mud-flats, estuaries and sea-cliffs; while, inland, there is an extensive industrial conurbation surrounded by mixed farmland, with long, low ranges of heathery hills beyond.

These hills (of primary interest to the walker) can be divided into three principal ranges. In the north-west are the southern slopes of the Cheviot Hills; to the south-west are the north-eastern hills of the Pennine Chain, and in the south-east are the northern slopes of the Cleveland Hills, on the edge of the Yorkshire Moors. These ranges are neatly partitioned. Between the Cheviots and the Pennines is a corridor of low land sloping east and west to either side of a low watershed called the Tyne Gap. From this point the River South Tyne flows eastward to Newcastle and the River Irthing westward towards Carlisle. Between the Pennines and the Cleveland Hills is a broader area of flat farmland. This is the northern end of a great swath of flat land which starts in the valley of the River Tees, narrows between the encroaching hills, and then opens out into the Vale of York to the south.

The Cheviots were formed by volcanic action. At their heart is the granite mass of The Cheviot (2674ft/815m). This is surrounded by an area of old red sandstone, between the River Till and Redesdale; while the lower hills at the southern end of the range are composed of carboniferous limestone.

Despite their volcanic source, the Cheviots lack the grandeur of the hills of the Lake District, Galloway or the Highlands; and here, the effect of the glacial activity of the Ice Age has not been to create knife-ridges and jagged peaks, but instead low, rolling hills divided by broad, shallow valleys. Only here and there does the rock extrude; as at the crags to the south of the Harthope Valley (3). This is not to say that the Cheviots are uninteresting, however. Once up amongst the hills the broad vistas of round-backed hills are extensive, and the walking is generally splendid.

The hills are largely covered by wide expanses of heather moorland and rough grassland, with peat bogs underlying the vegetation on many of the ridges. In the south, however, large areas of the hills have been given over to the huge conifer plantations of the Kielder Forest (16).

The watershed of the Cheviots forms the central section of the Scottish Border (11). A number of small rivers empty from the English side of the hills; notably the College and Harthope Burns (3,4), and the Rivers Breamish (10), Aln, Coquet, Rede and South Tyne. The College, Harthope and Breamish all ultimately empty into the River Till. (The rivers of the Cheviots tend to change names abruptly and often. The Till, effectively, is the Breamish by another name; while the Harthope and College Burns have become the Wooler Water and the River Glen respectively by the time they join the Till.) The Till then meanders through a wide, flat valley running north from the handsome market town of Wooler – the only settlement of any size in the northern Cheviots - to join the River Tweed.

The Pennines, to the south of the Tyne Gap, are more populous. The numerous small towns and villages in the northern dales – principally the valley of the South Tyne, Allen Dale, the Derwent Valley and Weardale – were primarily built to house the workers in the lead-mining industry, which flourished in the 18th and 19th centuries. As a result of the industry's decline, the population in the dales has not grown. This has had the pleasant side-effect of rendering modern building superfluous – the villages have generally been spared the doubtful attractions of modern additions, and have retained their original characters.

The principal towns and villages in the northern dales are Allendale Town (28) and Allenheads (29) (which has a small museum explaining its history) in Allendale; Blanchland (26) and Edmundbyers in the Derwent Valley; and the larger Wolsingham (31), Frosterley and Stanhope, plus others, in Weardale. In addition, the large industrial town of Consett – now bereft of its huge steelworks – sits on the edge of the hills by the side of the Derwent.

In general, the Pennines are less bleak than the Cheviots, and have a more pastoral air. This change is most marked in the southerly valley of Teesdale.

There were lead-mining settlements in Teesdale (notably at Middleton-in-Teesdale) but, in general, the valley is more agricultural than industrial. The main centre is the fine market town of Barnard

Castle *(36,37)*, situated at the point where the river debouches onto the plain; while further upstream there are numerous other, smaller settlements: notably Cotherstone *(35)*, Romaldkirk and Middleton.

In the Pennines, the volcanic rocks of the central Cheviots give way to limestones, sandstones and shales, but there are some intrusive rocks in Upper Teesdale; a fact which is partly responsible for the bleaker landscape around Cow Green Reservoir *(33)*.

Perhaps the best introduction to the landscape of the area is to drive along some of the high-level roads crossing between the dales, and linking them with Swaledale to the south and the pleasant town of Alston to the west. The views from these roads are magnificent.

The northern edge of the iron-rich Cleveland Hills *(39)* only just intrudes into the south-east of the area. This range is more properly a part of Yorkshire, to the south, but the manufacture of iron and steel had a great influence on the development of industrial Teesdale to the north, and industrial dormitory towns such as Loftus, Skelton and Brotton are reminders of the great days of this industry.

In addition to these three major ranges, there is a ridge of low sandstone hills curving south from Berwick, past Alnwick and on to Rothbury. In places, the sandstone has been raised up into dramatic ridges; notably at Thrunton *(13)* and the Simonside Hills *(15)*.

The major part of the population of Northumbria lives on the strip of flat land squeezed between these various ranges of hills and the North Sea. This band is generally only thin, but widens where it spreads up the floors of the larger valleys.

In north Northumbria, the flat land is largely given over to agricultural use. It starts in the north at the fine old town of Berwick: an important service centre for a large farming community on either side of the nearby Border. It is an architecturally fascinating place; principally because of the 16th-century town walls, but also because of the splendid town-houses and other fine buildings which are a testament to the historic wealth and importance of Berwick as a trading port.

Running south from Berwick, between the sandstone ridge and the sea, the narrow coastal plain is fringed with low cliffs and sand dunes. Eight miles (13km) south of the town is the tidal island of Holy Island (Lindisfarne) *(5)*, with its ruined priory and castle; reached by a road across a wide area of mud and sand at low tide. The castle sits on a ridge of basalt. This ridge is part of the Whin Sill: a dramatic ridge of intrusive volcanic rock which appears in a number of guises along the walks in this book. The Farne Islands are a manifestation of it, as also are the rocks on which Bamburgh *(6)* and Dunstanburgh *(8)* Castles are positioned, the ridge of Hips Heugh *(8)*, near Craster, the long ridges of Hadrian's Wall *(21)*, and the escarpments over which the waterfalls of Cauldron Snout *(33)* and High Force *(34)* fall.

There are a number of small villages spread along the coast to the south of Holy Island, including Bamburgh *(6)*, Seahouses, Beadnell, Craster *(8)* and Alnmouth *(9)* (on the small estuary of the River Aln). A few miles up the river is Alnwick – another fine market town, this time built up around the walls of Alnwick Castle. The town and the castle are both associated with the Percy family, Dukes of Northumberland. There is an 83ft/25m high monument to them at the southern end of the town, surmounted by the Percy lion, with its distinctive outstretched tail.

South-west of Alnwick, the ridge of sandstone hills re-emerges, running south-west towards Hexham *(22)*. The ridge gives way at one point, to allow the River Coquet to flow eastwards from the Cheviots, passing the town of Rothbury *(14)* at the narrowest point of the valley. At the mouth of the river are the port of Amble and the pleasant village of Warkworth, dominated by its splendid castle – another Percy stronghold, built between the 12th and the 16th centuries, now ruined and open to the public. The estuary is a popular haven for pleasure boats.

South of the Coquet, there is more farmland before, at the towns of Morpeth, Ashington and Newbiggin the built-up land around the mouth of the Tyne begins.

There are large settlements on the Tyne as far west as the old colliery town of Haltwhistle, near the Tyne Gap. To the east of this are the towns of Haydon Bridge, Hexham (with its fine old abbey) and Corbridge; while still further east, as the river leaves the hills, the more industrial towns begin: Prudhoe, Ryton, Blaydon and Newcastle itself. There is no need to describe Newcastle here; suffice to say that this fine city, at the heart of an extensive conurbation, is the most important centre in the area.

South of Newcastle, stretching down to the southern border of the area, is a band of mixed farmland and large towns; half on lumpy sandstone, and half on the southern end of a large coal deposit which stretches south from Amble to Bishop Auckland, and which was the historical basis for the establishment of heavy industry in the North East.

The main towns down the seaboard are Sunderland (at the mouth of the Wear), Peterlee, Hartlepool, Stockton and Middlesbrough (on the estuary of the Tees); while inland are Gateshead, Washington, Chester-le-Street, Houghton-le-Spring, Spennymoor, Bishop Auckland, Newton Aycliffe, Darlington, Durham and many others. Scenically, this area suffers from the disadvantages of any industrial area, but there are some gems amongst this mass of towns. The most notable of these is Durham (32).

Durham is the county town, and possesses a university, a castle and a cathedral. The tiny core of the town, with its narrow streets leading up a steep mound in a tight bow of the River Wear, is charming, while the centrepiece of the cathedral and castle is magnificent – one of the finest sights in Northumbria.

Excellent walks can be found throughout Northumbria but clearly, in an area of such diversity, the number of potential routes will vary from place to place. To some extent this fact is reflected in the choice of routes in this guide. Good walks are found in the greatest density in the Pennine and Cheviot Hills and along the Northumbrian coast, and these areas provide the majority of the routes included. This is not to say that there are not many more fine footpaths and Rights of Way throughout the entire region.

In addition to these, there are a number of established long-distance footpaths in Northumbria; some of which have been used in the routes in this book. The single longest path is the Pennine Way (11,21,27,33,34,38) but there are a number of shorter routes, including the Cleveland Way (39,40) (in the south-east of the area), the Weardale Way (30,31) (from Monkwearmouth to Cowshill), the Derwent Walk Country Park (25) (to the west of Newcastle), and the Waskerley Way, Brandon - Bishop Auckland Walk, Lanchester Valley Walk (32) and Deerness Valley Walk (a series of footpaths following the old railway lines to the west of Durham).

Details of all these routes are available locally.

History

The word 'Northumbria' instantly conjures up a number of isolated images: Durham Cathedral, Geordie coal miners, Holy Island and the intricate tracery of the Lindisfarne Gospels, the bare slopes of the Cheviots, a gaunt peel tower, Hadrian's Wall. In a way, this list provides a key to the major historic occurrences in the area. The wall represents the Romans, who annexed all of this area at one time or another, while Holy Island suggests the Anglo-Saxon Northumbrians who followed them, and the island's priory and intricate illuminated manuscripts represent the Celtic people who predated both invasions, and who returned to the island bringing the Christian religion with them – only to be evicted by the Vikings. Durham Cathedral also stands for Christianity – it is the burial place of St Cuthbert, the patron saint of Northumbria – but in addition represents the power of the Prince Bishops: a virtually autonomous power in the north, who existed as a buffer between southern England and the Scots. The peel (or pele) tower stands for the three centuries of continuous warfare which was fought along the line of the Scottish Border, while the bare Cheviots sum up the desolation in which these struggles occurred. And, lastly, the miner represents the coal-mining industry, which underpinned the industrial strength of the North East during the 19th century.

This last phase has had a more profound impact on the environment of Northumbria than all the others put together, and the coastal area, packed with towns, roads and industry, between the Tyne and the Tees, is one huge monument to the continuing Industrial Revolution. Nevertheless, throughout both urban and rural Northumbria, concrete references – churches, castles and monuments – remain to the sequence of invaders who arrived here, and to the roll of historical saints and villains who added colour to the region's past.

Perhaps the most important monument in Northumbria is Hadrian's Wall *(21)*; a unique legacy of the Roman conquest, and a structure of such antiquity that it seems almost a natural feature of the landscape.

The Romans first arrived in Britain in 55 BC, in the first of two military reconnaissances led by Julius Caesar. No invasion was intended at that time, but the opportunity was taken to establish trade and communication links between the Romans and the southern tribes of the Celtic peoples then inhabiting the British Isles.

About a century later, in AD 43, one of these southern tribes requested aid from Rome in a dispute against one of its neighbours. The new Roman Emperor, Claudius, decided that the time was right for an invasion. Using the squabble as a pretext, he sent four legions plus auxiliary troops (a total of around 50,000 men), under Aulus Plautius, to conquer the petty kingdoms of what is now Great Britain.

Not unnaturally, the invaders met with fierce resistance, and it was not until AD 80, under Agricola, that the Romans managed to subdue the land as far north as the River Tyne; conquering half the land of the Brigantes – a Celtic tribe inhabiting the land between the Forth and the Humber.

Initially, the Romans intended to subjugate the entire island, but in AD 86 one of the legions was removed from Britain for use elsewhere in the Empire. Now with only three legions at their disposal, the Roman leaders elected to consolidate

their grip on their existing possessions rather than attempt the dangerous business of extending them, and risk losing all in the process.

In AD 122 the Emperor Hadrian visited Britain, and initiated the building of the wall which was to bear his name. It was to act as a permanent northern line of defence for these possessions, and as a safe base for any future ventures into the shadowy north.

The wall was completed by AD 163. It is estimated to have been nine and a half feet (2.9m) in width and sixteen feet (4.9m) in height on its southern side, with a further four feet (1.2m) of breastwork to the north. It stretched 73 miles (117km), from the Solway Firth in the west to Newcastle in the east. To the north of the wall were a glacis (a shallow mound) and a ditch; along the line of the wall were sixteen forts, eighty smaller milecastles and 158 towers; and behind the wall were the Vallum (a large earthwork) and a military road.

For brief periods the northern frontier was moved northwards to the Antonine Wall, between the Clyde and Forth, but for the majority of the period of Roman occupation Hadrian's Wall remained the Empire's outer defence in Britain.

The wall was not an insurmountable obstacle to northern raiders, and was periodically breached or crossed by raiding tribesmen throughout the period of its defence. However, as long as the system of forts existed, and the soldiers to man them, the frontier could always be quickly restored against the limited forces of the northerners; particularly as they were primarily interested in booty (a characteristic which was to typify the Border tribesmen until the 17th century) rather than in the overthrow of the Romans, or any extension of their own territories.

This is not to suggest that the tribesmen were simply undisciplined barbarians, however. In AD 367 there was an attack upon the Roman forces in Britain which must have required considerable planning, and which was to have a great impact on the future of Roman Britain. In that year, there was a concerted attack upon the legions, not only by the Picts from beyond the wall, but also by the Saxons (from modern Germany) and the Celtic tribes of

Ireland. This simultaneous assault proved entirely successful, and although the tribes were eventually forced out of Roman Britain (heavily laden with their plunder), this attack, plus the mounting internal problems in the Empire as a whole, marked the beginning of the end for the occupation. In AD 410, the Romans finally cut all ties with their most northerly province.

The wall and its attendant buildings have largely been dismantled, and the stones used for other purposes; but the modern visitor may still see sections of the wall – particularly between Steel Rigg and Housesteads *(21)* – at least partially intact, and may visit the sites and ruins of the buildings. Of the latter, the best examples in Northumbria are the forts at Housesteads, Corbridge, Chesters – five miles (8km) north of Hexham – and Chesterholm – south of Steel Rigg – and the Mithraic Temple at Carrawbrough – three miles (5km) west of Chesters.

A further reminder of the Roman presence in England is provided by the roads; in this area principally Dere Street (from York, through Corbridge and into Scotland), Devil's Causeway (from Corbridge to Berwick), Maiden Way *(27)* (from York to Hadrian's Wall), and Stanegate, which predates the wall, and shadows its route from Newcastle to Carlisle.

The fate of Britain following the departure of the Romans, and its colonisation by the Anglo-Saxons, is most famously related in the Venerable Bede's *Ecclesiastical History*. Bede was one of the great Northumbrians. He was born on Tyneside in 673 and spent most of his life at the priory at Jarrow (much of which still remains, including sections dating from Bede's lifetime). When he died he was buried at the priory, but his bones were subsequently removed to Durham Cathedral.

According to Bede's *History*, the Roman retreat left the Celtic Britons of southern Britain open to further attacks from Ireland, the north and the continent. A certain King Vortigern, dismayed by continuing attacks by the Picts (from north of the wall) invited the Anglo-Saxon peoples to settle in Britain, on the understanding that they would aid the Britons in repulsing the raiders. In 449 three long ships duly arrived with a contingent of Anglo-

Saxons led by the brothers Horsa and Hengist. Having seen off the northerners they promptly turned upon their hosts, whom they also defeated. Having thus established a toe-hold in the east of England, they encouraged other German tribesmen to join them in this new, fertile land.

The dates in Bede's story tally with the available archaeological evidence, but the true history is presumably more complex. The pagan warriors of the Germanic tribes had been raiding in Christian Britain for many years, and must have been aware of the retreat of the Romans, and of the opportunity this gave them for conquest and colony.

Three distinct tribes colonised England: the Angles, the Saxons and the Jutes, of whom the Angles are held by Bede to have been responsible for the conquest of Northumbria. Once again, the truth must have been more complicated, but these raids had taken place only 250 years before the *History* was written, and oral tales of those stirring times must have persisted.

The kingdom of Northumbria originally comprised two smaller kingdoms: Bernicia in the north (stretching from the Forth to the Tyne), and Deira in the south (from the Tyne to the Humber). These two kingdoms were united as Northumbria under King Ethelfrid – of the Bernician royal line – in 603. Ethelfrid's main stronghold was on a great rock by the North Sea. This he named 'Bebba-burgh', after his wife, from which comes its modern name, 'Bamburgh' *(6)*.

In 616 the surviving heir to the royal line of Deira, Edwin, returned to Northumbria and took the kingdom from Ethelfrid. He brought with him a Christian wife from Kent, and adopted the religion himself. This ushered in a brief Christian era, which was ended by Edwin's defeat, and death, at the hands of the pagan King Penda of Mercia, in 632.

When Edwin had taken the throne of Northumbria, Ethelfrid's son, Oswald, had fled into exile. When he learnt of Edwin's death he swiftly returned, defeated a pagan army which was ravaging Northumbria, and took the throne himself.

It should be noted that, during Edwin's reign, Northumbria had become the most influential of all the Anglo-Saxon kingdoms; a position of ascendancy which Oswald was able quickly to re-establish.

Oswald had spent his years of exile on Iona and, when he gained the throne, he invited St Aidan to establish a monastery on the island of Lindisfarne (later 'Holy Island') *(5)*. This mission was a great success; the whole of Northumbria was soon converted and a number of monasteries were established in the area. Indeed, Northumbria was soon not only the political centre of Anglo-Saxon Britain, but also a major centre for religion and learning – the greatest examples of Northumbrian scholarship being the works of the Venerable Bede, and the splendidly illuminated Lindisfarne Gospels.

Initially, the religion was that of the Celtic church, as taught in Iona; but after the Synod of Whitby, in 664, the Northumbrian church accepted Roman practices, and the Celtic church swiftly declined.

Apart from St Aidan, two further important figures from the early Anglo-Saxon church deserve a mention at this point: St Cuthbert and St Wilfred.

St Cuthbert was born in the Lammermuirs (now in south-east Scotland, but then in northern Northumbria) and brought up in Melrose. When he was young he moved south to Lindisfarne, and eventually retreated to the Farne Islands to become a hermit. He remained on his island until King Egfrid persuaded him to become Bishop of Lindisfarne, in 685. After only two years, however, Cuthbert returned to his island and soon afterwards died. He was buried at Lindisfarne and when, after eleven years, his body was disinterred in order to have his coffin replaced, it was found to be uncorrupted. This curious fact, along with his appealing piety, made the name of Cuthbert revered in the North East, and he is now remembered as the patron saint of Northumbria.

Amongst Cuthbert's contemporaries was St Wilfred, who is best remembered for the foundation of Hexham Abbey *(22)* in 674. Part of the Anglo-Saxon structure of Hexham remains to this day, while other surviving examples of Anglo-Saxon Church building can be seen at St Peter's church at Monkwearmouth (east of Sunderland), Jarrow, Seaham Church (south of Sunderland) and Escomb Church (west of Bishop Auckland). In addition, the ruins of St Oswald's Chapel can be seen at Bamburgh Castle *(6)*.

This golden age of Christian learning and building, and indeed the brief era of Northumbrian domination of Anglo-Saxon Britain, came to a swift and decisive conclusion during the late 8th and 9th centuries: the period of Viking expansion.

The Anglo-Saxons were as unprepared for the coming of the Vikings as the Britons had been for their own arrival, 350 years earlier. Once again, the Christian land was overrun by a heathen invasion; indeed, by warriors who, ironically, worshipped the same gods whom the Anglo-Saxons had forsaken. Once again it was a series of swift and unexpected sea-attacks which proved irresistible. Indeed, the numerous religious centres along the North Sea coast – the repositories of much of the kingdoms' wealth – might have been situated solely to facilitate the plundering of these sea-rovers. The loathing with which the churchmen of the period spoke of the Vikings, tells us a great deal about their fear and helplessness.

The first attack came in 787, and the entry in the *Anglo-Saxon Chronicle* (a contemporary and generally sober record) for 793, when the Vikings returned, gives a flavour of the impact of this baleful turn of events.

'This year dire forewarnings came over the land of the Northumbrians, and miserably terrified the people; these were excessive whirlwinds, and lightnings; and fiery dragons were seen flying in the air. A great famine soon followed these tokens; and a little after that, in the same year, on the 6th before the Ides of January, the ravaging of heathen men lamentably destroyed God's church at Lindisfarne through rapine and slaughter.'

These attacks were rare and sporadic at first, and the Vikings would withdraw after each raid, but from the middle of the 9th century onwards they began to colonise; eventually founding an extensive kingdom – the Danelaw – centred on York, and extending as far north as Northumbria.

One curious side-effect of these raids was the founding of Durham *(32)*. In around 875 the monks on Lindisfarne finally decided that the island was untenable and fled inland; taking with them the body of St Cuthbert. For a century, the body was carried around Northumbria in search of a suitable resting place. For some years the saint was left at Chester-le-Street, before the monks finally decided to build a church for him on the site of modern Durham. The bones were placed in their present resting place, in Durham Cathedral, in 1104.

The Viking kingdom was eventually amalgamated into England, but for the remainder of the period of Anglo-Saxon rule they consitituted an important political and military presence in the north of England. The most important influence of this presence was that it separated the Anglo-Saxons of Lothian from their kin to the south. This brought Lothian under the influence of the Celtic kings of Scotland, and by the end of the 10th century the Scots had been able to extend their possessions as far south as the Tweed. Thus, the presence of the Vikings may be said to have reinforced the division of the island which had first been established by the Romans.

Following the successful Norman invasion in 1066, England came under the strenuous rule of William the Conqueror. His reign established a more profound geographical unity in England than had previously been the case, and this in turn brought the matter of the Anglo-Scottish relationship to the fore. Almost immediately, the Border became the scene of fierce warfare, with Malcolm Canmore of Scotland harrying Northumberland – ostensibly in support of his brother-in-law, Edgar Atheling, an Anglo-Saxon rival for William's throne.

Malcolm continued his campaigns against the English until 1093, when he was killed at Alnwick (Malcolm's Cross is a little to the north of the town). Curiously enough, in the same year he had been one of three dignitaries who had each laid a foundation stone for Durham Cathedral (the building of which was completed in only forty years). The other two men involved in the ceremony were the Prior and William de Carileph: the first Prince Bishop of Durham.

The Prince Bishops were a Norman invention. Having put down all independent power in the north of England, they discovered that the resultant vacuum led to instability, the virtual inability to administer law, and a potentially fatal weakness on the Scottish frontier. In 1091 William Rufus decided to establish the County Palatine of Durham; in effect creating a minor kingdom in the north, governed by the Bishops of Durham. The bishops governed from their hill above the River Wear: their twin authorities made concrete in the cathedral and the castle. They were answerable only to the King of England, and within their own lands their powers were regal: they could raise armies, create barons and coin their own money.

This ploy was to prove a remarkable success; with the bishops proving themselves capable of defending England against the Scots on a number of occasions, and never once – despite their potential for mischief – putting an army in the field against an English king.

The office of Prince Bishop lasted, a cheerful anachronism, until 1836, when the remaining powers of the office were transferred to the crown.

Whatever their successes, the bishops could never guarantee peace in the north. In the early part of the 12th century, with England in a state of civil war, David I of Scotland took control of Cumbria and Northumberland; that is, as far south as the River Tyne. The English took these possessions back within a few years, but the debate over the ownership of the counties fuelled many subsequent raids and battles.

The violence along the Border reached a new high during the Scottish Wars of Independence: an orgy of raid and counter raid, theft and bloodshed, which began in 1296, when John Balliol rose against Edward I, and ended, theoretically, in 1328, when Edward III signed the Treaty of Northhampton, recognising Scottish Independence. In truth, the matter was never truly laid to rest until 1603, when James VI of Scotland added the crown of England to his own, following the death of Elizabeth I.

In the intervening years, the Border region was in a state of perpetual uproar. It seems to have suited both governments to retain a political no-man's land between the two kingdoms. At any rate, nothing material was ever done to alter the situation; indeed, with the adoption of the *Leges*

Marchiarum - Border Laws - the violence was virtually institutionalised.

The situation was this. Scotland and England existed in a state of mutual mistrust. To the English, Scotland was a draughty back door, through which enemies could be expected to step at the most inconvenient moment; while to the Scots, England was a large and powerful neighbour whose expansionist urges were a perpetual threat to the very existence of their nation. Any build up of force on either side of the Border would be taken as provocation, and yet to leave it undefended was to invite disaster.

Neither government was subtle enough to have created the anarchy along the Border intentionally but, once it had been established, neither was particularly inclined to eliminate it. Thus there grew up, on either side of the line, a society which existed almost entirely for and by theft ('reiving' in the dialect) and blackmail. The Border was thus guarded on either side by fully armed, professional fighting men, who, if not exactly patriotic, were at least jealous of intrusion into their territory. To Edinburgh and London the virtual loss of an area of grey, heathery hills was a small price to pay for a continual watch along the marches, and it is worth noting that, at whatever cost, this bloody membrane successfully filtered all but the largest incursions in the following centuries.

The Border Law was first established in the 13th century, and amounted to an Anglo-Scottish agreement for (theoretically) cross-Border assistance in the policing of a defined area. On either side of the line, three March areas were delimited: the West, Middle and East Marches. The area covered in this book includes the land of the English East March (running south from Berwick to a line running approximately between The Cheviot and Alnmouth) and Middle March (the remainder of north Northumberland, running south to a line between Weardale and Newcastle). Each March had a March Warden, who was responsible for the maintenance of law in his area, and was expected to co-operate with his fellow wardens on both sides of the Border.

Once an independent law had been established to govern the Border area, it quickly developed idiosyncrasies. For example, reiving was so commonplace that the rights of pursuit ('trod') were firmly defined, and the victim of a raid had a legal right to pursue its perpetrator (even across the Border), and, effectively, to exact whatever revenge he felt most suitable. It is also worth noting that murder was not a capital offence in the Marches until 1560. It was simply too commonplace an occurrence to merit such distinction.

In these conditions, the Borderers developed into an insular breed. Cross-Border marriages were unlawful, but continued anyway, and many Borderers would cross and recross the Border as their safety or profit dictated. Many of the great families extended on both sides of the line and, in such a society, to belong to a great family was more important than to belong to a particular country.

At the heart of the culture was the raid: a horseback foray, generally at night, of small groups of well-armed reivers in search of livestock, victims for kidnapping, or some act of revenge in one of the endlessly complex family feuds which developed.

The only defences against such raids were either superior numbers of fighting men or defensible buildings. There were some large castles along the Border (notably Norham *(1)*, Berwick, Bamburgh *(6)*, Alnwick and others), but the more typical Border stronghold was the peel – a crude, narrow defensive tower, of which many examples can still be seen throughout the north – while in Northumberland a curious hybrid called a 'bastle' developed; a two-story defensive farm. A good example of a bastle can be seen at Black Middens *(17)*, near Bellingham. Another building worth visiting is the 14th-century Manor Office at Hexham *(22)*: at one time the local gaol, but now the Tourist Information Office

There is not space here to list the characters involved in these years of carnage, or the numerous tales of forays and skirmishes which characterised the period (the books *The Steel Bonnets* by George MacDonald Fraser and *The Border Reivers* by Godfrey Watson are recommended), but three major battles within this area should be mentioned.

The first was at Nevilles Cross *(32)*, Durham, in 1346. King David II of Scotland had ridden into England to create a diversion to help Philip IV of France (1346 was the year of the English victory at Crécy, at the start of the Hundred Years War). However, he was soundly defeated by an army of northern churchmen and nobles (led by Lord Percy and Lord Neville – two fine Northumbrian names) and spent the next 11 years as a prisoner in England.

In 1388 another Percy, Sir Henry, nicknamed 'Hotspur', took part in one of the most famous of Border battles, at Otterburn in Redesdale. The battle took place by moonlight, and proved a decisive victory for the numerically inferior army of the Scots, although their leader, James, Earl of Douglas, was killed. The battle was politically irrelevant, but was immortalised in the Border Ballads of the period.

By far the most important clash, however, was that at Flodden, south-east of Coldstream, in 1513. As at Nevilles Cross, the Scots took to the field at the request of the French, who were being pressed by Henry VIII; and, as in 1346, it ended in disaster for them. The Scots were defeated by an army led by the Earl of Surrey, and the Scottish king, James IV, was killed amidst the general slaughter.

The violence was finally ended by the accession of James IV's grandson, James VI of Scotland, to the throne of England. He showed no mercy to the reivers. The Border Laws were repealed, and the task of bringing the long backlog of malefactors to book began. Some joined the army, or bought immunity by turning against their neighbours; those who did not were either hanged or deported – many ending up in Virginia, or in the protestant colony in Ulster.

Within seven years there was peace along the Border for the first time in three hundred years; a peace which, largely, has lasted to the present day.

From that time onwards the main strand of Northumbrian history was the history of industry: its slow beginnings, swift growth during the 19th century, and gradual decline during the 20th.

The four industries which have had most impact upon the North East and its environment have been coal-mining, lead-mining, shipbuilding and iron and steel working; and of these, perhaps the most significant in the area's industrial development has been coal-mining.

Coal had been extracted from Northumbria's extensive deposits in a small way for several centuries before the invention of coal-driven steam engines, in the 19th century, encouraged landowners and entrepreneurs to invest in large-scale extraction.

One side-product of the industry was the development of the railways. The mining companies exported the coal by shipping it from the major rivers: the Tyne, Wear and Tees. In order to do this they had to transport the coal from the pits to the riverside staithes. This they did by the use of wagonways, along which horse-drawn wagons carried the coal. In time these wagonways were given wooden tracks (the first of these is believed to have been built in the Newcastle area during the reign of Charles I); later to be replaced by iron.

One of the most famous of these tracks was that between Wylam Colliery and Leamington (a small port on the Tyne) *(23)*. On this line William Hedley's pioneering locomotive *Puffing Billy* pulled coal wagons in 1813. By a strange coincidence, George Stephenson was born in a small cottage by the side of this track. Stephenson went on to design the locomotive which drew the train along the Stockton and Darlington line (opened in 1825), and also the famous *Rocket* which was used on the Liverpool to Manchester line.

In the dales of the Pennines a more important industry was lead-mining; the scale of which can be seen by the number of ruined mines and buildings which scatter the landscape. At Killhope, in upper Weardale, there are a number of renovated mine buildings, centred on a large waterwheel (30ft/9m in diameter). The wheel powered the machinery which crushed the lead ore, separating the lead from the surrounding rock.

A third important mineral-extraction industry was started in the area with the discovery of ironstone in the Cleveland Hills in the mid-19th century. This industry was largely responsible for the rise of the town of Middlesbrough, near the mouth of the Tees.

With coal, lead and iron to be exported from the area, local businessmen soon turned to shipbuilding as a logical expansion. With Britain's huge empire in its heydey, and trade flourishing, it proved to be a shrewd, and profitable, decision. Indeed, in the boom years of North East shipbuilding, the area was producing almost half of the world's output of ships.

All of these industries are now either finished or in decline. The boom period for Northumbria was very short – starting in the 19th century, and already drawing to a close by the 1920s. Nonetheless, within this short period the nature of the area had been completely altered.

When the Industrial Revolution began, it coincided with a population explosion. The new labour-intensive industries soaked up most of the local increase in people, and then, still being short of manpower, began to attract others from outside the North East. Large areas of poor-quality housing were quickly built to house them. These towns, and their 20th-century successors, are the legacy of that boom period.

Those who are interested in Northumbria's industrial past may wish to visit the Open Air Museum at Beamish (on the A693 between Stanley and Chester-le-Street). The museum attempts to recreate life in the North East around the turn of the century. It includes furnished shops and buildings, operational transport, a colliery village and a farm. A short walk to the north of the museum is Causey Arch; built in 1727 and believed to be the oldest railway bridge in the world.

Those who prefer to think of the region as it was before its industrial development may be more interested in Cherryburn (near Prudhoe, on the River Tyne): the birthplace of one of England's finest rural artists, Thomas Bewick.

Bewick was born in 1753, and died at Gateshead in 1828. He was buried in the graveyard at Ovingham Church, having spent most of his life in Northumbria. His highly detailed woodcuts of birds and animals, and tiny vignettes of country life are both wonderful works of art and fascinating illustrations of rural Northumbria two centuries ago.

Place Names

Though the various peoples who invaded and colonised Northumbria in distant centuries have left little in the way of physical reminders of their presence, the extent of their habitation within the area can still be divined – if somewhat crudely – by the local place names.

Some of these names date back to Roman and Celtic times, but such names tend to be rare, and much altered by usage. As a result, the most interesting place names in rural Northumbria (the more modern names in the industrial heart of the area come from a wide variety of sources) tend to be either Anglo-Saxon or Scandinavian. That is to say, they were coined by either the Anglo-Saxon tribes who invaded England after the retreat of the Romans (principally the Angles in Northumbria), or by the Vikings who, in turn, invaded the land of the Anglo-Saxons.

In the first surge of the Viking colonisation of Northumbria, the resident Angles were displaced,

and a community which spoke only its own Scandinavian tongue, and created purely Scandinavian place names, was established. Gradually, however, the two peoples became more intermingled, and the descendants of the Vikings began to use the Anglian language – albeit spiced with Scandinavian borrowings – which in turn developed into the Northumbrian dialect of today.

Thus there are three recognisable stages in Northumbria's Anglian/Viking place names. The pure Anglian, the pure Scandinavian, and the subsequent blend. Examples of the first group can be found throughout the region, but predominate in the north of Northumberland, where the Viking colonisation was latest and numerically weakest. The distribution of pure Scandinavian names is exactly the opposite, and they can be found in greatest profusion in the county of Durham. Blended names exist throughout Northumbria, and their existence lends uncertainty to the provenance of many of the others, since amongst the Scandinavian words which became part of the Anglian language were such common place name elements as 'dale', 'beck' and 'fell'. The existence of these elements in a name cannot, therefore, be taken as final proof of Viking settlement.

Some other elements – such as 'howe' and 'toft' – existed in both languages (both came from the same Germanic root), and thus place names including these elements are of a similarly uncertain racial source.

The list below gives translations of the more common place name elements in Northumbria. Where the elements are known to be of either Scandinavian (s) or Anglian (a) origin (subject to the provisos above) this is indicated.

Many of these elements appear in wildly differing forms throughout the area. Do not be put off by seemingly eccentric spelling.

Common Elements in Place Names

Beck - *Stream* (scandinavian)
Brig - *Bridge*
Burn - *Stream* (anglian)
-by (suffix) - *Scandinavian farm or settlement*
Common - *Area of land open to usage by all the residents of a specified town or parish*
Cleugh - *Ravine or valley*
Clint - *Rocky cliff*
Cote - *Place for animals*
Currick - *Heap of stones*
Dale - *Valley* (s)
Dean - *Small valley*
Dod/d - *Rounded hill-top or buttress*
Fell - *Hill* (s)
Force - *Waterfall* (s)
Garth - *Enclosure, yard or garden* (s)
Gate - *Road, path, street*

Gill - *Ravine or wooded glen; small stream* (s)
Grain - *Branch of stream or valley* (s)
Grange - *Farm or barn*
-ham, ingham (suffix) - *Anglian farm or settlement*
Haugh - *Riverside meadow*
Heugh - *Crag, ravine or valley*
Holm - *Rich, flat land by river* (a)
Hope - *Farmland at valley head*
Howe - *Low hill*
Knowe - *Low, round hill*
Lea, lee, ley - *Forest glade or open country*
Linn - *Waterfall* (a)
Mire - *Bog* (s)

Moss - *Bog* (a)
Pike - *Sharp-pointed hill*
Rig/g - *Ridge or long, narrow hill*
Scar - *Bare hill-face or cliff* (s)
Shaw - *Wood* (a)
Shield, shiel - *Temporary dwelling by high, summer pasture*
Spittal - *Hospital, often for foul diseases*
Side - *Slope of hill*
Sike, syke - *Small stream or ditch*
Tarn - *Small mountain lake* (s)
Thwaite - *Clearing or meadow* (s)
Toft - *Homestead*
Wick - *Farm* (a)

Natural History

There is a wide variety of natural habitats in Northumbria, ranging from the damp moorland of the Cheviots and Pennines, through the sheltered dales and eastern farmland, to the raw North Sea coast, with its mud flats and sand dunes. Within this area there are two large Nature Reserves – the mud flats and dunes of Lindisfarne and the open moorland of Upper Teesdale – but, outside the heavily built-up area around the mouths of the Tyne, Wear and Tees, the greater part of Northumbria is pleasantly rural, and a sighting of some interesting species can generally be anticipated along any of these routes.

Given the variety of habitats, it would be meaningless to list the species present without also specifying the type of place where they might be found. Therefore, the area has been divided into a number of environments which recur along the routes – **Commercial Forestry, Woodland, Hills and Moorland, Farmland, Freshwater, Seashore** – and the bird, animal and plant life typical of each then listed. Routes which particularly feature each type of environment are listed beneath the headings. Naturally, it is impossible to be entirely accurate with such a brief study, and great good fortune is required to see some of the less common species, but this should give a rough indication of the type of thing which may be seen along the way.

Commercial Forestry
(4,7,12,13,14,15,16,17,22,24,27,36)
There was little coniferous woodland in Northumbria until commercial forestry began in the 1920s. Now, there are a number of large forests throughout the area, and one positively huge one at Kielder, on the southern hills of the Ceviots. These plantations are of comparatively little interest to naturalists. They provide cover for **rabbit, fox, red** and **grey squirrel** and **roe deer**, but the trees are generally packed close together, thus keeping sunlight from the forest floor and inhibiting the undergrowth necessary to sustain the smaller animals and insects at the bottom of the food chain.

The trees planted are quite varied and can include **Scots** and **lodge-pole pine, Sitka** and **Norway spruce, Japanese** and **European larch, Douglas fir** and others.

The species of birds which it may be possible to see within the plantations include **crossbill, siskin, goldcrest, coal tit, redpoll** and **long-eared owl**, although sightings can often be difficult through the close packed branches.

Woodland
(18,22,24,25,26,36,39)
The original forest of broad-leaved trees which once covered much of Northumbria has now virtually disappeared. The main forests are now those of commercial conifers, and the largest remaining patches of broad-leaved woodland are generally either in deep river valleys (where grazing animals are unable to reach the young trees, and the land was not considered worth

clearing) *(18)*, in fenced parkland, or on the verges of railway lines *(25,27)*, although small patches can be found along most of the routes in the book.

Where such woodland does exist, it can provide the richest of inland habitats. Common species of trees throughout Northumbria include **oak, hazel, beech, yew, ash, hawthorn, sycamore** and others, with **alder, sallow** and **willow** in riverside woods *(19,31,37)*. These provide a breeding ground for insects (the oak being particularly rich in this respect) which in turn attract birds such as **pied** and **spotted flycatchers, green** and **great spotted woodpeckers, treecreeper, willow warbler** and **blackcap**. Other woodland species include the **wren, blackbird, song thrush, blue tit** and **great tit**, plus birds of prey, such as the **sparrowhawk** and **tawny owl**, which prey upon the smaller birds and mammals.

Woodland mammals include the small **mice, voles** and **shrews**, and the larger **fox, badger, hedgehog** (these three, being largely nocturnal, are rarely seen) **red** and **grey squirrel, roe deer, weasel** and **stoat**.

As long as a wood is kept free of heavy grazing, it should also contain a large number of wild flowers; attracted by the rich soil created by the falling leaves from the trees. Common species include the **foxglove, primrose, wood sorrel, lesser celandine, wood anemone, wild garlic, violet** and **bluebell**.

Hills and Moorland
(2,3,7,11,13,14,15,26,27,29,31,33,34,38)
Although there are no hills above 3000ft/900m in Northumbria, and thus none of the more mountainous environments which can be found in Scotland and the Lake District, the low, rounded hills of the Cheviots and the Pennines provide a large area of grass and heather moorland. The moor is often balanced on a layer of peat: a mass of black, half-rotted, sodden vegetation which can be badly eroded along the routes of footpaths.

Sheep will often be found grazing on the moors, but the primary use of these areas is generally as grouse moors. Each spring, areas of heather will be burnt from the moors to encourage new growth, which, in turn, encourages the **red** grouse. This bird will be met on virtually any high-level walk, and is usually seen springing up from the heather with a loud, chuckling cry. For game birds they often seem ridiculously tame.

A rarer resident of the high ground is the **peregrine falcon**; a masterful flyer which takes its prey – up to and including the grouse in size – on the wing. Other birds of prey include the **merlin** (a much smaller falcon which mainly feeds on small birds such as the **meadow pipit**) and the **hen harrier**, while the **short-eared owl** – the only British owl which can regularly be seen by day – can sometimes be seen hawking over the moors in search of small mammals.

Other birds to be found on the moors include the **blackcock, snipe, curlew, lapwing, carrion crow** and **wheatear**.

On heather moors the usual cover is of **ling heather**, while on damp patches of the moors there are **bog cotton, bog asphodel, bog mosses, cranberry** and others. In Upper Teesdale *(33)*, however, the cover is sufficiently different to have warranted the setting up of a Nature Reserve. In this area, the 'sugar limestone' soils are unable to support trees. Woodlands have never developed, and, as a result, some of the plant species which are found here have been present since the end of the last Ice Age. These include subarctic species such as the **spring gentian, Teesdale violet** and **alpine forget-me-not**.

Farmland
(1,4,8,9,17,19,20,21,28,30,35,36,37,38,40)
Farmland takes up a huge proportion of Northumbria. On the flat areas by the coast the land is almost entirely arable, while on the inland hills it is a mixture of arable and grazing and, in the highest areas, the land is almost entirely given over to grazing; particularly sheep grazing. With all this variety, it is difficult to generalise about species. However, plants which may be found throughout the farmland include **coltsfoot, dandelion, scabious, birdsfoot trefoil, cowslip, bugle** and **tufted vetch**.

Many of the lower fields are lined with hedges, which encourage **finches, sparrows, robin, linnet, wren, blackbird, thrushes** and others; while larger

birds include **magpie, lapwing, curlew, snipe** (these last two particularly in the higher fields) **pheasant** and **partridge**; plus **redwing, fieldfare** and **waxwing** in the winter months. Of birds of prey, the one most often seen in farmland is the **kestrel**.

There are few mammals which are specific to farmland but watch out for **stoat, weasel, fox, rabbit** and **brown hare**.

In Northumbria there is one semi-domesticated species deserving of mention: the **wild white cattle** of Chillingham Castle (south-east of Wooler). This small herd is considered to be the purest remnant of the cattle of Bronze Age England.

Freshwater
(1,4,10,16,18,19,28,30,31,33,34,36,37)
This grouping is rather broad; covering everything from upland bogs to wide rivers and lakes.

The water arrives as rain, mostly in the hills, and seeps into the peat where it forms bogs and shallow pools, surrounded by the **bog cotton, bog mosses** and other plants of the damp moors. This water leaves the moor in one of the countless narrow, overgrown sikes and gills which drop down from the hills, slipping along the floors of broad valleys, gouged out of the hills in the Ice Age. These streams gradually become larger as they converge and combine.

In the upper waters, the most common birds are the **dipper** and the **grey** and **pied wagtails**, which feed off insect larvae in the streams, as do the tiny **trout** which can often be seen in the larger pools.

Often these waters will flow through narrow, wooded valleys. In such places, the **kingfisher** may be seen, while more open water may attract the **heron, coot, moorhen, dabchick** and **great-crested grebe**.

A number of varieties of duck can be found by Northumbrian waters, including the **goosander, mallard, teal, shoveler, tufted duck** and **pochard** during the summer months.

There are few mammals which specifically live by the water, but both the **otter** and the **mink** – an import from Canada which has escaped and become naturalised – are present in this area. The former is very rare, and neither, being shy and largely nocturnal, are likely to be seen.

Seashore
(5,6,8,9,40)
Any naturalist thinking of the Northumbrian coast thinks immediately of the Farne Islands: a small archipelago, the nearest islands of which are only two miles (3km) offshore from Bamburgh *(6)*. These small, rocky islands are incredibly rich in breeding seabirds – including **puffin, guillemot, kittiwake, fulmar, razorbill, cormorant, shag** and **eider duck** – while also having a colony of **grey seals**. Boat trips are organised to the islands from Seahouses. Information on these can be obtained locally.

The mainland coast can be divided into three main types of environment: mudflats, sand dunes and cliffs.

The first type is not heavily represented in Northumbria, but there is a small area of tidal mud at the mouth of the River Tees, and a larger one around Holy Island *(5)* and Budle Bay *(6)*, incorporated into what is now the Lindisfarne National Nature Reserve.

The mudflats are of particular interest for the large numbers of wildfowl and waders which are able to feed on the weeds, shellfish, worms and crustaceans which congregate in and on the mud. Wildfowl which can be seen during the winter months include **mallard, teal, wigeon** and **pintail; grey-lag** and **pale-bellied brent**. While, of waders, there are **greenshank, redshank, curlew, whimbrel, sanderling, little stint, bar-tailed godwit, dunlin, knot, oystercatcher, turnstone** and others.

As well as mudflats, the Nature Reserve includes large areas of sand dunes, both on the island and on the mainland. These moving masses of loose sand are bound together by **marram grass**, while other plants to be found in this dry environment include **hound's tongue, viper's bugloss** and **bloody cranesbill**. Holy Island also has breeding colonies of **little** and **sandwich terns**.

Other stretches of dunes can be found along the Northumberland coast: notably at Beadnell Bay, Alnmouth Bay *(9)* and Druridge Bay.

There are few cliffs along the Northumbrian coast, but there are some low ones to the south of Craster *(8)*, and some very high ones – over 600ft/ 180m – on the south Cleveland coast *(40)*.

General
The walker is unlikely to come to any harm from the wildlife of the area, as long as common sense is employed and birds and animals are not too closely aproached. There is one poisonous snake in the area – the **adder**. It is rare to see one – usually coiled in a patch of sunlight, somewhere quiet – and rarer still to be bitten. Adders are extremely shy and will always move away if they sense someone approaching. Anyone who is bitten should consult a doctor. Bites are not lethal, but they give rise to an unpleasant, temporary illness.

Bulls are very common throughout Northumbria, and anyone walking in the area will confront one from time to time. They appear, and generally are, extremely lethargic. However, anyone who takes liberties with their good nature is asking for trouble.

Advice to Walkers

Always check the weather forecast before setting off on the longer walks – particularly those in the higher hills of the Cheviots and Pennines – and prepare yourself for the walk accordingly. Remember that an excess of sunshine – causing sunburn or dehydration – can be just as debilitating as snow or rain, and carry adequate cover for your

body when on the hills.

Snow cover on the higher slopes (which can linger into the spring) should be avoided by inexperienced walkers as it often covers hidden pitfalls which are likely to cause injury. Also, when soft, snow is extremely gruelling to cross and can sap the energy very quickly.

The other weather-associated danger on the hills is mist, which can appear very swiftly and cut visibility to a few yards. Such conditions should be anticipated, and a map and compass carried while on the higher hills. Visitors to the Cheviot and Pennine hills sometimes fail to realise just how difficult navigation amongst the mass of similarly rounded peaks and buttresses can be, even in clear conditions.

Obviously these problems are unlikely to arise on the shorter, simpler routes, but it is always wise when out walking to anticipate the worst and to be ready for it. The extra equipment may never be needed, but it is worth taking anyway, just in case. Spare food, a first-aid kit, a whistle and a torch with a spare battery should be carried on all hill walks. In addition, details of your route and expected time of return should be left with someone, whom you should advise of your safe return.

There is one final danger for hill walkers which is entirely predictable. From August onwards there is grouse shooting on the moors. If you are planning to undertake one of the hill routes then check with the local estate or tourist office before doing so, thereby avoiding a nuisance for the sportsmen and possible danger to yourself.

Please note: all the routes in this book follow either rights of way or other agreed paths. You are asked to stay on these paths and not to venture onto the surrounding land, unless along another right of way or in an area of agreed general access.

Country Code

All walkers, when leaving public roads to pass through farmland, forestry or moorland, should respect the interests of those whose livelihoods depend on the land. Carelessness can easily cause damage. You are therefore urged to follow the Country Code:

Guard against all risk of fire
Keep all dogs under proper control
 (especially during the lambing season -
 April/May)
Fasten all gates
Keep to the paths across farmland
Avoid damaging fences, hedges and walls
Leave no litter
Safeguard water supplies
Protect wildlife, wild plants and trees
Go carefully on country roads
Respect the life of the countryside

1 Norham

Length: 2 miles (3km)
Height climbed: Negligible
Grade: C
Public conveniences: Norham
Public transport: Norham is on the bus route
between Berwick and Kelso

*A short walk along a rough path between
farmland and the riverside, returning on a
quiet public road.*

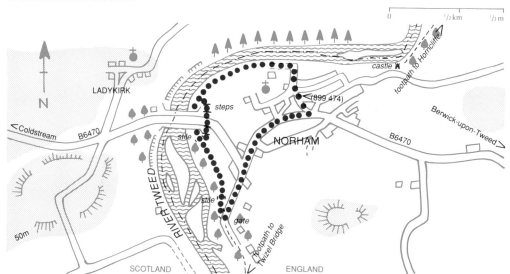

Norham is a small village by the River Tweed,
chiefly famous for its fine 12th-century castle, built
by the Bishop of Durham. Norham Castle – now a
stately ruin on a mound above the river at the
eastern end of the village – was one of the major
English strongholds along the Border, and
witnessed a great deal of fighting during the
centuries of Anglo-Scottish warfare.

For this walk, park in the centre of Norham –
eight miles (13km) south-west of Berwick on the
A698/B6470 – and walk down the track from the
village green to the river. Once at the river, turn
left, along what starts as a wide, clear track. The
Border runs along the centre of the river at this
point, so the steep bank on the far side of the water
is in Scotland.

When the track ends, continue along a rough
path. Looking back, there is a fine view of the

castle while, to the left, the parish church is visible
across the farmland. Parts of the original Norman
church remain, but considerable rebuilding was
undertaken in the 17th and 19th centuries.

Continue along the river bank until the bridge is
reached. Either climb up the steps and cross the
road, or else follow the path under the four-span
bridge and then cut left, over a stile, to rejoin the
correct path; running beside a fence to the right of a
field above the river.

Near the end of the field there is a stile over the
fence to the right. Cross this and then continue to a
gate onto the road. Turn left to return to Norham

There are additional footpaths by the river:
westwards (turn right at the road) to Twizel Bridge,
and eastwards (from beyond the castle) to
Horncliffe and beyond.

2 Doddington

Length: 4 miles (6.5km)
Height climbed: 450ft (140m)
Grade: B
Public conveniences: None
Pubic transport: Bus services from Berwick and Wooler

A circuit on rough paths and quiet roads, crossing open grazing land and fields.

To reach the little village of Doddington, drive three miles (5km) north of Wooler on the B6525. The cluster of houses sits on the edge of the broad flood plain of the River Till, tight under the lee of Dod Law: a small, rounded hill.

Park in the centre of the village and start walking up the road signposted to Wooler Golf Course. After 100 yds (90m), turn hard right over a stile by a sign for 'Dodlaw'. The path beyond is not clear. Follow the fence to the right until a line of hawthorn trees appears up the slope to the left. Climb up to this line and follow it to a fence. Cross the stile and carry on to the last hawthorn, a short distance ahead. Cut left from the tree, up a clearer path, to the top of the slope; then turn right, below the low wall of an Iron Age fort. The views across the valley from this stretch are very fine.

Continue along the path to Shepherds House. Pass in front of the cottage and then turn left, up the side of the little field behind. When the field ends, ignore the clear track ahead and cut half right, up on to the golf course.

The route is a little difficult at this point. Cut right towards a low ridge. Climb this and walk past the golf tee beyond to a stile over a fence. Beyond is an area of heather moorland. Head half left along a clear track, towards a small stand of conifers, visible about half a mile (1km) to the north-east. Walk to the left-hand side of the plantation and follow the wall which continues beyond it until it reaches a stile. Cross the stile and cut left, with a dyke to the left, for about 100 yards (90m) to another stile. Cross this and turn right, down through The Ringses – another Iron Age fort – and on to a track along the bottom of the slope. Cut left along thc track to return to Doddington.

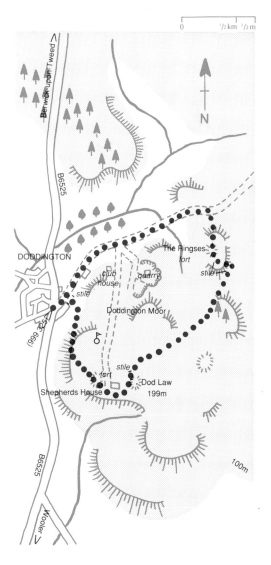

3 Harthope Valley

Length: 5¹/₂ miles (9km)
Height climbed: 750ft (230m)
Grade: B
Public conveniences: None
Public transport: None

A steep climb over rough tracks and open moorland, leading to fine views. Return by a low, riverside track.

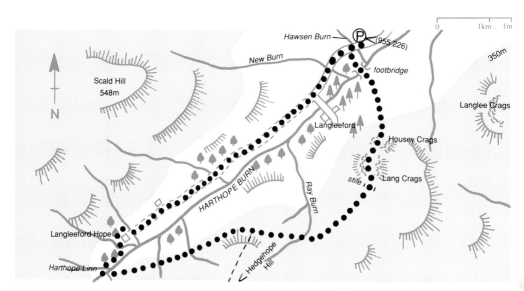

This walk climbs into the hills to the south of the upper waters of the Harthope Burn. To reach the start of the route, leave Wooler along Cheviot Street, turn right at the first junction and continue to Middleton Hall, then turn right up the road signposted to Langleeford. Three miles (5km) up the narrow road there is a small car park at the foot of the Hawsen Burn, which flows in from the right. On the far side of the burn is a sign for a footpath to Housey Crags.

The crags are visible ahead: rocky eminences rising above the scrub woodland by the water side. Follow the footpath down to the burn and cross the wooden footbrige. Start climbing beyond. There are a number of rough paths on the steep slope, but the route is obvious enough: aiming slightly to the left of the crags. The views from the summit are excellent: eastwards across farmland to the sea, and

westwards to the Cheviots; indeed, The Cheviot itself is almost due west, at the head of the valley.

Walk west from the crag to the northern end of Long Crag; then cut left, down the length of the rocky ridge; then right, over a stile, and on across open, marshy moorland near the watershed of the hill.

As the path approaches Hedgehope Hill, it bears left and starts to climb towards the summit. For this route, drop down to the right of the path and skirt around the lower slopes of the hill (there is no clear path). The cottage of Langleeford Hope is visible in a stand of trees on the far side of the burn, and a short distance upstream is the wooded gorge of Harthope Linn. Aim to join the burn a little above the gorge. Cross the burn and walk back down the far side of the valley, returning to the start of the route along a footpath, which first becomes a track and then a metalled road.

4 Happy Valley

Length: 4 miles (6.5km)
Height climbed: 250ft (80m)
Grade: B
Public conveniences: None
Public transport: None

A circuit on rough tracks and quiet roads around a quiet valley; out through grazing and farmland and back along the flood plain.

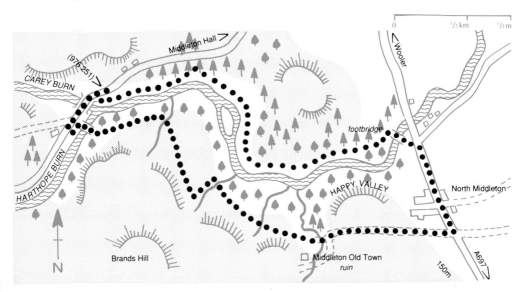

To reach Happy Valley, leave Wooler along Cheviot Street and continue along the minor road beyond. Cut right at the first junction, then follow the road to Middleton Hall before turning right on the road signposted for Langleeford *(3)*. Park in a space to the right of the road, a little after it joins the burn.

Walk on along the road, towards the bridge across the Carey Burn. Cross this and then turn hard left, beside a fence; then left again, over a stile; and then right, across a footbridge over the Harthope Burn. Climb the slope beyond and walk on, with an oak wood spreading down the valley slope to the left.

When a fence comes in from the right, go round it and cut right, on a well-trodden path. Continue in this direction until a dyke and a line of hawthorns cross ahead. Turn left, and follow the

dyke to the foot of the field; then turn right, through a gate, and follow the path beyond along the edge of the valley, towards a plantation. Cross the stile to the right of this and continue, keeping the trees to the left. At the end of the trees cross another stile and continue with the fence to the left. At the end of the field cross a further stile, and then a footbridge. Climb the slope beyond to join a track. Turn left to reach Middleton.

Once the track reaches the road turn left, as far as the ford over the burn. To the left of the ford is a footbridge. Cross this and turn left, along a clear track through dense conifer and broad-leaved woodland by the burn side.

When the woodland ends continue across the grazing land on the flood plain, back to the bridge. At one point the burn swings to the north, and it is necessary to follow a path through the gorse scrub up to the right.

5 Holy Island

Length: 3¹/₂ miles (5.5km)
Height climbed: Negligible
Grade: C
Public conveniences: Holy Island
Public transport: Bus service between Berwick and Holy Island

A circuit of a tidal island on rough paths and tracks, passing a ruined priory, a castle, sand-dunes and coastal-scenery.

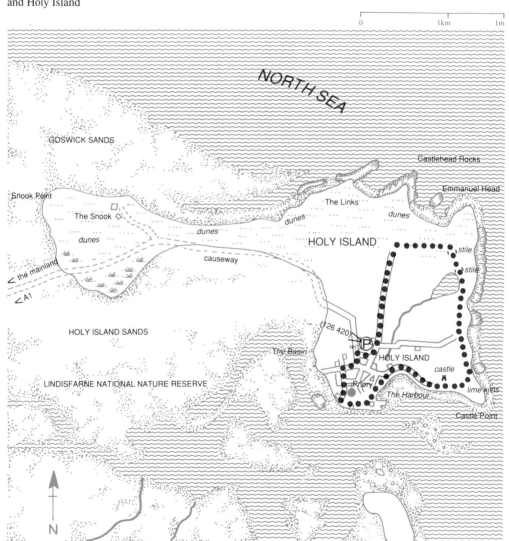

Holy Island, or Lindisfarne, is a small, square island; little more than a mile (1.5km) square, with one long, sandy promontory, the Snook, reaching out westwards towards the mainland. There is one small village on the island, a ruined priory, a harbour and a small castle, perched on a rocky, abrupt ridge.

Stripped to such bare details the island may not sound too exciting, but it is a place of unique beauty, and of enormous historical importance. Indeed, it holds a place in English religious history which parallels the importance of Iona in Scotland.

It was from Iona that the earliest Celtic missionaries came to the island. King Oswald of Northumbria, during a period of misfortune, spent a number of years in exile in Scotland, during which time he was converted to Christianity. When he had re-established himself at Bamburgh *(6)* (a short distance to the south, along the coast), he sent to Iona for a missionary. In 635 St Aidan arrived and established a mission on Holy Island, within sight of his patron's castle.

The mission was spectacularly successful, and remained a centre of religion and learning until, in June 793, the Vikings arrived. In this and subsequent raids the Christian centres in Northumberland were effectively destroyed. An attempt was made to rebuild the church on Holy Island, but by 875 the situation had become impossible and the island was deserted.

Following the period of Viking rule the island was reinhabited by a cell of Benedictine monks, at the end of the 11th century. It was they who built the priory – dedicated to the most famous Bishop of Lindisfarne, St Cuthbert. The building survived the ravages of the Border wars, before falling during the dissolution of the monastries, in 1541, at which time much of the stone was removed for use in the construction of the castle – intended as a further defence against the Scots.

Holy Island is only an island for around half of each day; the rest of the time it is joined to the mainland by a road across a mile (1.5km) long causeway over the wide sands and mud-flats which are now incorporated into the Lindisfarne National Nature Reserve. Therefore, **it is important to check the local tide tables** (check at tourist information centres) **before planning a trip to the island.**

To reach Holy Island, drive eight miles (13km) south of Berwick on the A1 and then turn left along a minor road to the island. Once the village is reached, turn first left to the car park.

Walk out of the car park and turn right, then turn left at the first junction and right at the next, and walk on down the main street. Turn left at the end of the street and walk on, down the street, and along the lane beyond which passes the church and continues down to the shore. Turn left, along the shore, then climb up on to a low ridge along the southern edge of the island. From this point there are fine views in all directions.

Continue along the ridge until it drops down towards the harbour. Join the track which runs along the head of the little bay, past the row of upturned fishing boats which are now used as sheds.

On the north edge of the bay, the track joins a road leading out towards the castle – now owned by the National Trust and open to the public. Walk beyond the castle, past the old lime kilns, and join the track which curves to the left, inland from Castle Point, to shadow the eastern edge of the island.

Follow this track past a small lake. There is a stile across the track near the end of the lake. A short distance beyond, there is another stile. Cross this and then, after about 100 yds (90m), cut left along a grassy track. After a short distance there is a fork in this track: take the right-hand route.

Continue along this path, which runs along the edge of the sand dunes on the northern edge of the island. When the track reaches a junction, turn left and follow a straight track back into the village.

6 Bamburgh

Length: 5 miles (8km)
Height climbed: Negligible
Grade: C
Public conveniences: Bamburgh
Pubic transport: Bamburgh is on the bus route between Berwick and Alnwick

A coastal walk, largely across sand, passing a fine castle. Possible return by public roads.

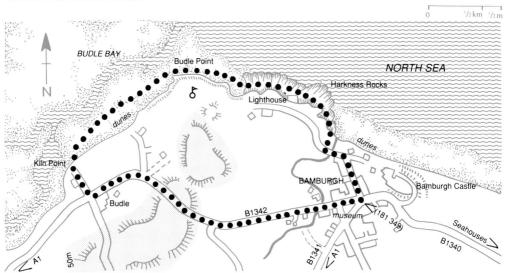

The little village of Bamburgh is dominated by its castle: a great mass of red sandstone on an abrupt dolerite rock above the North Sea. The rock has been used as a stronghold from at least Anglo-Saxon times, but the oldest section of the building still in use is the great keep, dating from the 12th century. Additions and repairs to the structure were still being made at the turn of the century. The castle is open to the public from Easter to October

To reach the village, drive south from Berwick, along the A1, for around 15 miles (24km), and then turn left onto the B1342.

Starting from the centre of Bamburgh, walk north on a street called 'The Wynding' to the edge of the village and then cut down to the sandy shore. If the tide is in, it may be necessary to follow the road, and the path beyond, a little inland from the coast; but otherwise it is best to walk along the

shore, across the sands and over the Harkness Rocks . Continue beyond, round the point to Budle Bay – a large tidal inlet of mud and sand, of particular interest for its sand dunes, and for the large numbers of wildfowl and waders which it attracts.

Either return by the same route or continue to Kiln Point and cut inland up the track to the B1342; cutting left along the path to the left of the road to return to Bamburgh. This is a pleasant enough walk, but the road can be busy during the summer, and should then be avoided.

Another attraction of Bamburgh is the charming Grace Darling Museum. The centrepiece of the collection is the coble (the traditional fishing boat of the North East) in which Grace and her father rescued the crew of the *SS Forfarshire* in 1838.

7 Ros Castle

Length: Up to 4¹/₂ miles (7km)
Height climbed: 500ft (150m) Undulating
Grade: B/C
Public conveniences: None
Public transport: Chillingham – two miles (3km)
from walk – on bus route from Alnwick to Wooler

A forest walk, on rough tracks and quiet roads, leading through conifers and open moorland to a splendid viewpoint. Shorter routes available.

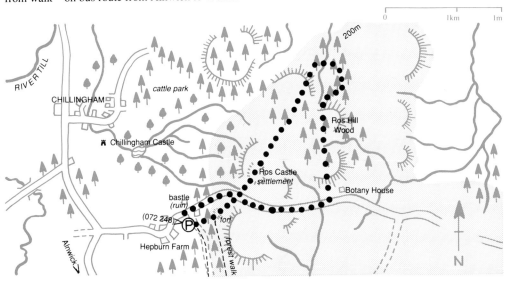

To reach this walk, drive nine miles (14.5km) north from Alnwick on the B6346 road to Wooler. When the road cuts left (signposted to Wooperton) carry straight on. After a little over a mile (1.5km), the road splits again. Keep to the right. After a further 1¹/₂ miles (2.5km) a road cuts up to the right, signposted to 'Hepburn Forest Walks'. Drive up this road for a little under one mile (1.5km) to a car park.

There are three signposted walks starting from the car park. Of the three, the most interesting is the longest: 'Ros Castle'.

Start walking uphill from the edge of the car park; through a band of trees and on, up a steep, rocky slope to the grassy mounds of an Iron Age fort. From this point there are fine views. To the west, just beyond the car park, is the ivy-covered ruin of an old bastle, with The Cheviot and its

surrounding peaks across the valley of the Till beyond. The land directly to the north, across the road, is the parkland around Chillingham Castle: the home of the famous wild white cattle.

Cross the fort and continue over the moorland beyond; following a clear path towards the heathery mound of Ros Hill. Cross the road and climb to the top of the hill, from where there is a view unrivalled in Northumbria: across low land to the coast, and including three great coastal castles – Lindisfarne *(5)*, Bamburgh *(6)* and Dunstanburgh *(8)*. There are boards at the summit, naming the prominent features of the view, plus a plaque commemorating Sir Edward Grey (Foreign Secretary, 1905-16).

From the summit, the path drops down and makes a well-signposted loop through the wood to the north, before returning to the car park along the public road.

8 Craster

Length: 4½ miles (7km)
Height climbed: Negligible
Grade: B
Public conveniences: Car park
Pubic transport: Craster is on the bus route
between Berwick and Alnwick

A circuit of rough footpaths and quiet country roads leading along a cliff-edged coast and through a hinterland of fields and woodland.

Craster is a picturesque little fishing village, about six miles (9.5km) north-east of Alnwick. A little over a mile (1.5km) to the north are the considerable ruins of Dunstanburgh Castle; easily reached from the village along a clear path.

For this route, park at the car park to the right of the single road to the village, just before it reaches the houses. Leave the car park along a footpath heading south-west. The path starts through scrubby woodland. After a short distance it splits. Follow the left-hand track, continuing inside the wood.

When the wood curves to the left, the path leaves it through a gate and enters a field. Head half right across the field; up a slight incline. Shortly, Craster South Farm becomes visible on the far side of the road ahead. Cross the road and continue up the road opposite. Turn half left after a row of cottages and climb gently uphill on a good track, with a hedge to the left. Continue through two fields, always approaching the rocky ridge of Hips Heugh. At the end of the second field, go through a gate and cut to the right, skirting around the edge of the dolerite crags, and continue, past two sycamore trees, to a stile over a dyke to the right. Cross this and head half left, towards a gate to the left of a belt of woodland.

Continue along the right-hand edge of two fields, with woodland to the right, before cutting sharp right, along a track through a gap in the trees, and on to a public road.

Cut left down the road for half a mile (1km) until it makes a right-angled turn to the left. Walk straight on down a track signposted to Craster and then turn left along the cliffs, rocks and sandy inlets of this fine coastline, back towards Craster. The path enters the village by the children's playground at the end of Heugh Road.

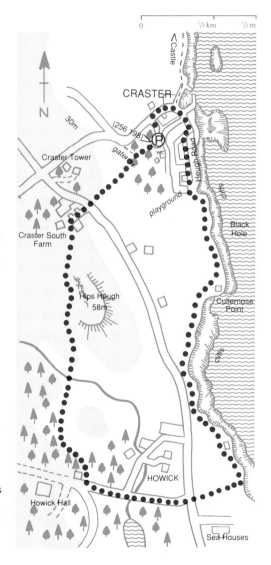

9 Alnmouth

Length: 4 miles (6.5km)
Height climbed: Negligible
Grade: C
Public conveniences: Alnmouth
Pubic transport: Alnmouth is on the bus route between Newcastle and Alnwick

A circuit on public roads and footpaths, leading through open farmland, and along a muddy estuary and a fine sandy beach.

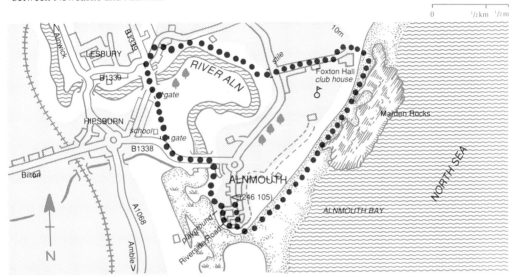

Alnmouth is a fine sea-side village on a peninsula between the tidal mud of the Aln estuary and the sands of Alnmouth Bay. In mediaeval times it was an important port, but now it is simply an unspoilt haven for small boats.

Walk down to the southern end of the village and turn right along Riverside Road. Continue on this road until, just beyond a children's playground, a path cuts to the left along the mud-flats. Follow this to the Duchess's Bridge, then climb up onto the bridge and turn left.

Walk along the road for about a quarter of a mile (0.5km) until, a short distance before the school, a small gate opens into a field to the right. Walk along the right-hand edge of this field, and then continue on a path parallel to a row of houses which starts to the left. Opposite the end of the row there is gate, after which the path cuts half left, leading across a field to another gate. This leads to

a road, and then to a bridge over the Aln.

Cross the bridge and follow the track beyond into the village of Lesbury, and then turn right along the road. When the B1339 cuts left carry straight on for a short distance and then cut right along the footpath signposted for Foxton Hall. Follow this path between two houses and into a field.

Cut half-right, down to the river; following the path through three fields before climbing the steep slope to the left, slightly to the right of a line of telegraph poles. Once at the top of the slope, cross a stile, and the road beyond, and walk down the driveway into Alnmouth Golf Club, directly opposite.

Follow the drive down to the club house. When a wall starts on the left-hand side, walk down a path to the left of it, leading down to a fine sandy shore, and then turn right to return to Alnmouth.

10 Ingram

Length: 7¹/₂ miles (12km)
Height climbed: 550ft (170m) undulating
Grade: A
Public conveniences: Ingram and riverside (see map)
Public transport: School bus service from Wooler

Circuit on public roads and rough footpaths along riverside and across high moorland. Some navigation necessary.

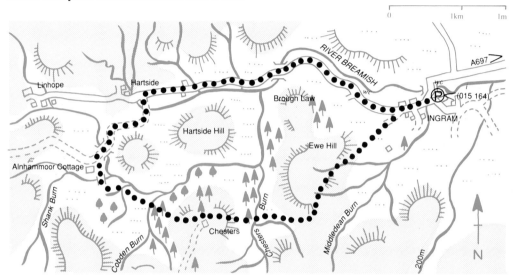

Ingram is a small hamlet in the lovely Breamish Valley. To reach it, drive eight miles (13km) south of Wooler on the A697 road, then turn right up a minor road for a little over two miles (3km). There is a car park at the information centre in the village, but it is possible to park virtually anywhere by the riverside.

Walk three miles (5km) up the road to Hartside, then cut left at the sign for a footpath to Alnhammoor.

Follow a good track down to the river and cross a bridge. About 100 yds (90m) beyond the bridge cut left, along a grassy path, with Alnhammoor Cottage up to the right, to a gate in a dyke. Go through this gate and turn left towards another gate. Once through this second gate turn right, over a footbridge across the Shank Burn. Bear left to a further gate and then start walking around the edge

of the two fields beyond, to a conifer wood which climbs the steep slope beyond the Cobden Burn.

Enter the wood through a gate and follow the path beyond, leading through the trees and on up the slope beyond to Chesters, at the right-hand edge of a conifer plantation. Go through the gate behind Chesters and set off across the field beyond. There is no clear path, but a band of woodland is visible ahead, on the near side of a valley. Down the far slope of the valley is a tributary valley. Head towards this, passing through gates on either side of the plantation.

Start walking up the left-hand side of the valley ahead (there is no path). When the burn starts to bend to the south, carry straight on; over the ridge of the hill (leaving the summit to the left); then bear left, down the slope above the Middledean Burn to join a track leading back down to the road.

11 Windy Ghyle

Length: 8 miles (13km)
Height climbed: 1200ft (360m)
Grade: A
Public conveniences: None
Public transport: None

A long, moorland climb on rough, damp tracks onto open hilltops. Heavy going and exposed, but fine views.

Along its central section, the Border follows the watershed of the rounded, heathery Cheviot Hills. This walk involves a short stretch along this exposed boundary, above the headwaters of the River Coquet.

To reach the start of the walk, turn up any one of the roads off the A697/B6341 between Wooler and Otterburn which is connected to the network of little roads leading west to Alwinton, and then follow the road beyond along Upper Coquetdale (a good road map is absolutely essential to find this route). Seven miles (11km) up the valley there is room for parking; a mile (1.5km) beyond the school at a split in the road.

Go through the gate at the foot of the ridge between the two roads and start walking up the bridleway beyond. After a steep climb there is another stile. Cross this and cut right, then just carry on walking up the undulating ridge until it reaches the watershed – three miles (5km) from the start – and the fence which runs along the Border.

Cut right and follow the fence to Windy Ghyle: visible ahead, topped by the cairn named after Lord Francis Russell who was killed on the hill in 1585. To reach the cairn, cross a stile over the fence near the start of the final ascent. The views from the top are spectacular.

Cut right from the cairn, through a gate in the fence, and on to a heathery ridge. There is no clear path at this stage. Drop down the slope to the left of the ridge until a track appears ahead, running down to the right along a further ridge between the Trows and Wardlaw Burns. Follow this clear path down to the meeting of the waters just above Trows Farm, and then continue down a good road through an idyllic little upland valley back to the start of the walk.

12 Alwinton

Length: 6 miles (9.5km)
Height climbed: 900ft (270m)
Grade: B
Public conveniences: None
Public transport: Bus service between Alwinton and Rothbury

A brisk climb along good tracks (wet in places) across moorland and through conifer woodland.

To reach the little village of Alwinton, turn on to any one of the minor roads to the west of the A697/ B6341 between Wooler and Otterburn which joins the network of minor roads around the upper waters of the rivers Aln and Coquet. Alwinton is the last settlement of any size on the Coquet.

Park in the car park at the western end of the village. Walk eastwards, across the village green and the footbridge over the Hosedon Burn beyond, then cut left up a good track. Continue climbing on this track – an old drove road called Clennell Street – until a large conifer plantation comes into view.

Follow the track around the left-hand edge of the plantation to the ruin at Wholehope. Go through the gate to the right of the building and cut half right across the field ahead to a small gate. Go through this and climb up to join a good track beyond. Turn right for a short distance, then left, up a rough path through the conifers. When the fence to the right ends, cut right for a short distance, then left, and follow the path down to the old shooting lodge at Kidlandlee.

When the path reaches the fields around the buildings, go across a stile and down a narrow field between two dykes. Cut right, through a gate, just before a shed is reached; then left, through another gate, to join a good track. Follow this down the hill from Kidlandlee, and when it turns to the right, go through a gate to the left and follow a rough path down the hill to the floor of the Alwin Valley.

From the end of the path cut right, along the bridleway which climbs up the side of the valley. Follow this track to the top of the slope, where it turns sharply right. Carry straight on until a gate becomes visible on the horizon. Cross the stile nearby, and another beyond, to rejoin the original track from Alwinton.

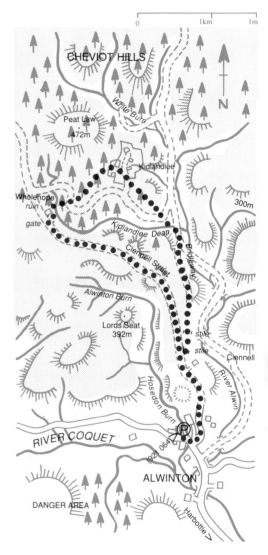

13 Thrunton Wood

Length: 2-9 miles (3-13km)
Height climbed: 740ft (220m)
Grade: A/B/C
Public conveniences: None
Public transport: Thrunton Brickworks – one mile (1.5km) from car park – on Alnwick-Wooler bus route

Four forest walks of differing length; the longest climbing along a series of ridges, offering fine views.

To reach Thrunton wood, drive seven miles (11km) south-west of Alnwick on the B6341 road for Rothbury, then turn right on the A697. Take the first turn to the left. This road is signposted for the forest, and a car park appears on the left after about two miles (3km).

Thrunton Wood – a Forestry Commission plantation consisting almost entirely of conifers – is planted on a series of great sandstone sheets which, following volcanic action, have had their edges raised as long ridges of steep cliffs. From the top of these cliffs there are fine views of the countryside to the north.

There are three forest walks through the conifers and along the ridges, each marked by posts of a different colour (see map), plus an archaeological walk, leading past bronze-age and 16th-century remains. For the longest and most interesting route – the red walk – leave the car park and turn left along the road. At the point where the road makes a hairpin bend to the right, carry straight on, along a good track.

The path is very clearly marked. It starts along a track beneath Thrunton Crag (passing, on this section, the end of a path leading up to Wedderburn's Hole: a cave used as a hideout by a reiver of that name). It then climbs over the pronounced hump of Castle Hill – topped by the remains of an Iron Age fort, and planted with old beech trees – before climbing up to Callaly Crag through an area of Pine forest, planted in the last century and now with the appearance of a natural wood.

Once on Callaly Crag, the path cuts right and begins a long circuit – once again, clearly signposted – of the new plantations to the west; following rough footpaths, and climbing along the clear ridge of Long and Coe Crags before dropping back down into the forest and returning to the car park.

14 Rothbury

Length: 5 miles (8km)
Height climbed: 500ft (150m) Undulating
Grade: B
Public conveniences: Rothbury
Public transport: Bus services from Newcastle,
Morpeth, Alnwick and local towns

*A circuit on rough paths and tracks across
open moorland and through conifer
woodland. Fine views.*

Rothbury is a pleasant country town, climbing up
the steep slopes on either side of a narrow stretch of
Coquetdale, some twelve miles (19km) south-west
of Alnwick on the B6341.

Start walking from the centre of the town.
Walk up Providence Lane (leading north from the
eastern end of the High Street), then continue up
the hill to join Hillside Road, on the northern edge
of the town. On the far side of the road, a sign
indicates a footpath to Cartington. Walk up the
path (carrying straight on between two fences when
the main track cuts right to a house), past the left-
hand edge of a conifer plantation and on to the
moor. Climb directly up the slope ahead to join a
track running across the hill towards the plantation.
Turn right along this track.

As it approaches the trees, a yellow arrow
indicates the start of a clear path leading off to the
left. Follow this path across an area of open
moorland towards another plantation. Cross a stile
into this plantation and turn right along a grassy
track. At a T-junction in the wood, cut right, down
to Primrose Cottage on the edge of the trees.

From the cottage, turn left on a clear track
running along the edge of the plantation, signposted
to 'Crocky's Heugh'. Continue along this track.
At one point it is crossed by another track: carry
straight on as before, now through woodland. At
the far end of the wood the track emerges once
more onto the moor. Initially it heads westwards,
towards another plantation, but then it cuts to the
south, winding across the moorland and providing
fine views of Coquetdale and the Simonside Hills
(15).

Continue on this track until it rejoins the path
from Rothbury, then turn right to return to the start.

15 Simonside

Length: Up to 4¹/₂ miles (7km)
Height climbed: 750ft (230m)
Grade: B/C
Public conveniences: None
Public transport: None

Three forest walks through conifer woodland and along a ridge of open moorland.

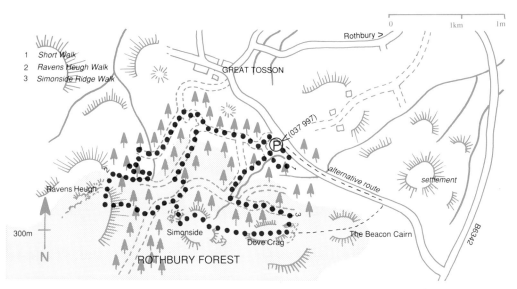

1 Short Walk
2 Ravens Heugh Walk
3 Simonside Ridge Walk

Rothbury is a fine old country town, in a narrow section of Coquetdale, pressed between a steep slope to the north *(14)* and the forestry covered slopes and ridges of the Simonside Hills to the south.

To reach the start of the forestry routes through the plantations on these hills, drive south from the centre of Rothbury on the B6342. Cross the mediaeval bridge over the Coquet and turn right immediately, onto a minor road. Continue along this road for a little over two miles (3km). At each junction, follow the signs for Great Tosson.

Turn left just before entering this tiny village. Follow the road until the forest starts on the right-hand side, then take the first turning to the right; signposted as a picnic place.

There are three routes through the forest, the two longest of which – the Ravens Heugh Walk and the Simonside Ridge Walk – lead up to the pronounced rocky ridges which rise up above the forest to the south. These ridges are of sandstone, and are similar in composition and form to those in Thrunton Forest *(13)* to the north.

The routes are well signposted, but there is one possible alteration to the paths indicated. The Simonside Ridge route climbs on to the ridge of heather and stone (from which there are fine views of Rothbury and Thropton, and of the hills to the north of Coquetdale) and follows it eastwards to Dove Crag. From this point, instead of following the forest walk back into the trees, continue along the ridge on the path to the Beacon Cairn, and from there drop down to the quiet road below. Turn left along the road to return to the start of the walk.

16 Kielder Forest

The map below shows the locations of seven established forest walks around the Kielder Reservoir. All the routes are comparatively short, and all are suitable for dogs. There are car parks and public conveniences at the start of each route. A bus service runs from Bellingham to Tower Knowe, Leaplish and Kielder Village. During the summer there is a ferry service between various points on the lake shore (see map).

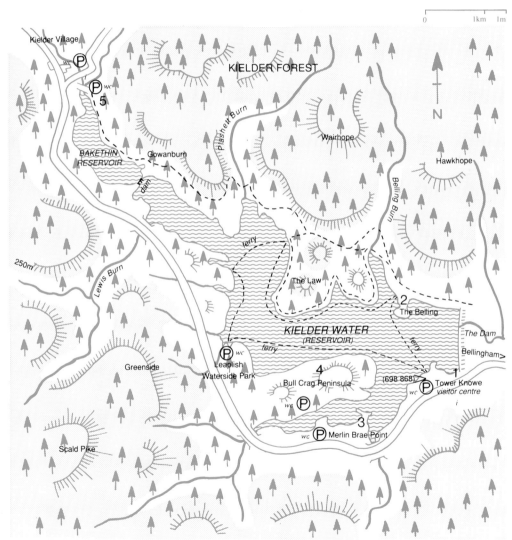

At the head of the valley of the River North Tyne, where the headwaters of the river are collected from the southern Cheviots along the Scottish Border, is the Kielder Water Reservoir. The reservoir was built to provide water for the north of England, and was completed in 1982. The dam is three quarters of a mile (1km) long, and contains 44,000 million gallons of water in an irregularly shaped lake with a surface area of 2,684 acres. This is the largest man-made lake in Europe.

Surrounding the reservoir is, fittingly enough, the largest forest in Britain. This too is man-made, and consists largely of ranks of identical conifers. Information can be found on both the reservoir and the forest at the two information centres, at Kielder Village (a Forestry Commission village at the head of the reservoir, built in the 1950s), and at Tower Knowe, near the dam (see map).

Further information is also available on the forest walks described below, in the form of a series of leaflets.

In addition to the signposted trails, there are a number of forestry roads, footpaths and bridleways around the reservoir. These include routes along the north side of the shore. There is no access for vehicles along the northern side of the lake but there is a ferry system which operates between the jetties along the shoreline. Some of these alternative routes are shown on the map.

To reach Kielder Reservoir, drive 16 miles (26km) north of Hexham on the A6079/B6320 towards Bellingham. Turn left before crossing the bridge into the village on a minor road. Follow this for a little over 10 miles (16km) to the dam.

Signposted Routes

1) Tower Knowe
Around two miles (3km). Starting at the Kielder Water Visitor Centre and passing through mixed woodland and open moorland along the water side.

2) The Belling
Around two miles (3km). Starting at Hawkhope car park at the northern end of the dam and passing through commercial forestry along the shore of the reservoir before continuing around a small promontory and returning to the car park past the entrance to the Falstone Mine: a drift mine for coal.

3) Merlin Brae
One and a half miles (2.5km). Starting from the Whickhope car park and passing through a mixture of forestry, woodland and grazing land. Provides a good view of the boats at the Whickhope Anchorage.

4) Bull Crag
Three miles (5km). Starting from the Bull Crag picnic site and viewpoint and passing through mixed woodland and moorland on a shoreline path around a promontory. Views across to the Whickhope Anchorage.

5) Bakethin North Shore
Around two miles (3km). Starting at Fishermen's car park and passing through a mixture of conifer and broad-leaved woodland along the edge of the little Bakethin Reservoir: a top-up reservoir for Keilder Water.

In addition to these five, there are two further, shorter footpaths, at Leaplish (the Beech Walk) and Keilder Village (the Duchess Trail).

17 Greenhaugh

Length: 6 miles (9.5km)
Height climbed: Undulating
Grade: B
Public conveniences: None
Public transport: Bus service from Bellingham to
Lanehead - one mile (1.5km) from Greehaugh

*A circuit on quiet country roads, through
moorland and farmland, with a short section
through conifer woodland on rough tracks.*

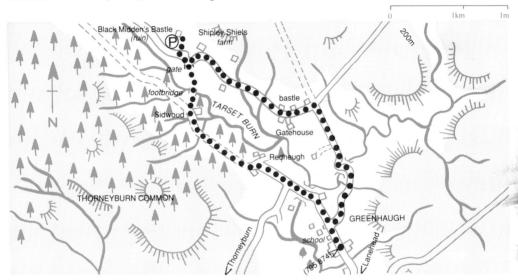

Greenhaugh is a tiny village on the Tarset Burn (a
tributary of the River North Tyne flowing out of
the eastern edge of Kielder Forest. To reach it,
drive three miles (5km) north-west from
Bellingham – 16 miles (26km) north-west of
Hexham on the A6079/B6320 – to Lanehead, on
the minor road up the North Tyne valley; then, at
the junction, cut right along another minor road for
one mile (1.5km) to Greenhaugh.

Park in the village and start walking northwards
along the road. Turn right at the first junction, then
follow the road for one mile (1.5km) to the next.
Turn left into Gatehouse. On the right-hand side of
the road, at the far end of Gatehouse, there is a fine
example of a bastle – a two storey cross between a
farmhouse and a peel, developed uniquely in
Northumbria during the late 16th and early 17th
centuries as a defence against the raids of the local

reivers.

Continue along the road for a little over a mile
(1.5km), until it makes a sharp bend beyond the
farm at Shipley Shiels. At this point, a gate leads
into the field to the left. This is the start of the
return path, but those who wish a closer look at a
bastle should continue along the road for a short
distance to a small car park. From this, a rough
track leads up a slope to the ruin of Black Midden's
Bastle. The roof and floors are missing from the
building but, otherwise, it is in good condition.

Return to the gate and set off across the field to
a footbridge over the burn. Climb through the
conifers beyond to join a forest track, then cut left,
past Sidwood and Redheugh, and on to the road.

Ignore the turn to Thorneyburn and continue,
back across the burn and on in to Greenhaugh.

Walk 17

18 Hareshaw Linn

Length: 3 miles (5km) there and back
Height climbed: 250ft (80m)
Grade: C
Public conveniences: Bellingham
Public transport: Bus service between Bellingham and Hexham

A short, lineal climb up a deep, wooded glen, leading to a dramatic waterfall. Paths generally good.

The small town of Bellingham is the main centre for a large area around the valley of the River North Tyne (on which it sits), Redesdale and the massive Kielder Forest *(16)*. The most interesting building in the town is St Cuthbert's Church. The earliest sections date from the 13th century, but later additions were made in the early 17th and the 19th centuries. The place is very strongly built, with a heavy stone roof and slit windows. The cannon balls found in the roof during its reconstruction are evidence that, this close to the Border, a building had to be strong to survive.

To reach Bellingham, drive 16 miles (26km) north-west of Hexham on the A6079/B6320.

From the centre of the town, turn down the road signposted for Redesmouth. The road crosses the Hareshaw Burn almost immediately. Cut left directly after the bridge on a road leading up to a car park on the edge of the town.

From the car park, a signpost indicates the start of the footpath. The route is quite clear. It starts by climbing through an area of open ground – the mounds under the grass are the remains of the 19th-century coal- and iron-mining industry – before entering the fine mixed woodland around the upper valley. The path winds back and forth across the burn on a sequence of footbridges before finally entering a rocky canyon at the head of the valley, with a fine waterfall of some 30 feet (48m) dropping through the gap between two great blocks of stone. At the end of the path a small cave is cut into the rocky wall to the right, providing a dry viewing point of this dramatic scene.

Return by the same route.

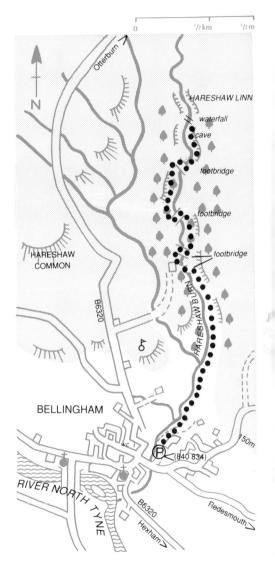

19 Bellingham Riverside

Length: 2-3 miles (3-5km)
Height climbed: Negligible
Grade: C
Public conveniences: Bellingham
Public transport: Bus service between Bellingham and Hexham

A riverside route on rough footpaths, running along the edge of the flat fields of the haugh. Return along a quiet road.

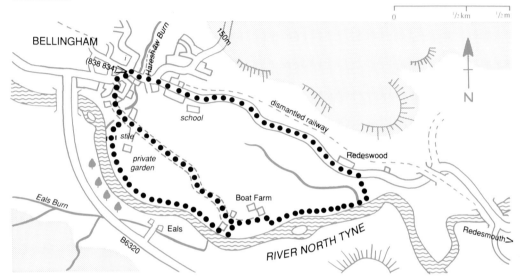

The little market town of Bellingham sits in the midst of some fine walking country, with numerous footpaths through Kielder Forest *(16)* to the west, and over the open moorland around Redesdale and the valley of the River North Tyne. In addition, there are a number of shorter routes nearer the town *(18)*, including this pleasant riverside stroll.

To reach Bellingham, drive 16 miles (26km) north-west of Hexham on the A6079/B6320. Park in the centre of the town and walk down through Manchester Square. Turn left from the square down a small lane, leading to a bridge over the Hareshaw Burn. Cut left across this, then hard right, down a footpath along the side of the burn. After a short distance, the path veers to the left and crosses a stile into a private garden, with the River North Tyne now down to the right. Stick to the path across the garden, then carry on along the

riverside beyond. The path is narrow, and can be overgrown during the summer, but the route is quite clear.

Continue along the river until a gate leads on to a farm access road by a small wooden house. At this point, it is possible to shorten the route by turning left down a track back into Bellingham, making a walk of two miles (3km). Otherwise, turn right along the road. Pass Boat Farm on the left, and continue until a gate, directly ahead, leads into a field. Ignore this and walk between the fence, to the right of the gate, and the river.

Continue along this narrow path until it crosses a small burn. Just beyond this, turn left across a field and then climb the bank beyond to reach a minor road. Turn left along the road to return to Bellingham. Listen out for traffic, as the road is rather narrow in places.

Walk 19

20 Wark

Length: 8 miles (13km)
Height climbed: Many steep undulations
Grade: B
Public conveniences: None
Public transport: Wark is on the bus route
between Hexham and Bellingham

*A circuit on quiet public roads through an
area of hill-farmland and woodland.*

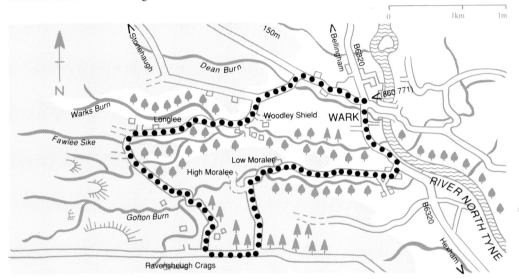

This pleasant route exclusively follows public
roads, and is included partly because it passes
through some fine countryside, and partly as an
example of the excellent walking to be had on
minor roads throughout the area. These roads are
often, as in this case, little more than metalled farm
tracks; unfenced and crossed by field gates. Any
brief study of a detailed map should suggest
alternative routes of a similar nature.

For this route, drive 10 miles (16km) north
from Hexham on the A6079/B6320 and park in the
little village of Wark by the River North Tyne.
This tranquil group of grey buildings, clustered
round a central green, was a centre for Scottish
government of the area in the 12th and 13th
centuries.

Start walking westwards, along the road
signposted to Stonehaugh. After the houses end
there is farmland on either side and a small burn

down to the left. At the first junction, keep to the
left, on the Stonehaugh road.

Follow the road down across the Dean Burn
and then continue to the next junction. Cut left
once again, this time on the road signposted for
Longlee. The road drops down into the valley of
the Warks Burn, crosses the burn on a small bridge
and then climbs up the far side, passing the farm at
Longlee. It then makes a steep hairpin bend to the
left and continues to climb up to an area of high,
reedy pastureland.

Follow the road up to the next junction, with
the stone ridge of the Ravensheugh Crags ahead
and to the right. Cut left along a straight road, then
first left again to drop down into the valley of the
Gofton Burn. The road turns right beyond the burn
and follows it for a mile (1.5km) above the slope of
a fine, wooded gorge, before jinking left to join the
B6320. Turn left to return to Wark.

21 Hadrian's Wall

Length: 1) 4$\frac{1}{2}$ miles (7km); **2)** up to 7$\frac{1}{2}$ miles (12km)
Height climbed: 1) 425ft (130m) undulating; **2)** steep undulations
Grade: A/B
Public conveniences: Once Brewed

Two reasonably easy walks on footpaths, tracks and quiet public roads; both running beside sections of Hadrian's Wall.

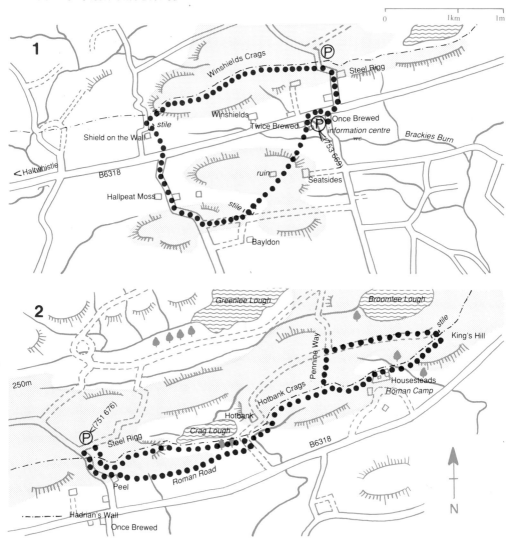

When Hadrian's Wall was completed, in AD 163, it stretched 73 miles (117km), from the Solway Firth in the west to the Tyne estuary in the east. For most of the following two centuries, it was to be the northern boundary of the Roman Empire in Britain.

The builders' search for the most easily defended route for their wall led them across the bleak land to the north of the River South Tyne, where they were able to utilise the outcrops of the Whin Sill, a recurring geological feature in Northumbria which produces a series of steep crags. Thus, the wall is not only a relic of great archeological interest, it is also scenically fascinating.

The two walks described below both follow well-maintained stretches of the wall along its highest sections, providing both an idea of how the wall must have appeared when it was complete, and fine views across the low hills to north and south. The two routes join at Steel Rigg, and can either be walked individually or as a single route of some 12 miles (19km).

1) This route starts from the information centre at Once Brewed. To reach the centre, drive to Haltwhistle – 16 miles (26km) west of Hexham on the A69 – turn north on a minor road to join the B6318, then turn right for two and a half miles (4km).

From the centre, walk across the B6318 and then up the minor road opposite to join the wall on a low ridge. Once on the ridge cut left, over a dyke and on along the footpath signposted to Shield on the Wall. The path follows the line of the wall and crosses Winshields Crags – the highest point on its route.

After 1³/₄ miles (3km) the path is crossed by a public road. Turn left for a short distance, then left again, across a stile over a dyke. Cut half right beyond; heading towards the left-hand end of the dyke extending from Shield on the Wall Farm, visible below. Walk past the the end of the dyke and on down to the B6318. Cross the road and continue along the quiet road opposite.

After a little under a mile (1.5km) the road bears right and a clear track leads off to the left. Walk along the track until it reaches the junction with the track to Bayldon. Climb over the stile to the left and walk half-right across the field beyond, climbing onto a low ridge from where a ruin is visible in a stand of trees.

Cross the stile to the right of the ruin, into a narrow field. Head for the stile half way down the right-hand side of the field, then continue past the ruin at the foot of the next field to the footbridge over Brackies Burn. Climb the slope beyond to join the road a short distance to the west of Once Brewed.

2) This route starts from the car park at Steel Rigg. To reach it, follow the driving instructions given above for Once Brewed, then turn left, up the minor road along which the first route starts. The car park is to the right of the road at the brow of the ridge.

Walk east from the car park. The path starts on the top of the wall, then drops down and continues beside it; along the crags of Steel Rigg and through the woods above Crag Lough. At the far end of the lough, the path crosses the track leading back to Hotbank Farm. At this point it is possible to double back to the car park, by turning right down the track for a short distance, and then right again at the sign for a footpath, along the Roman road. This makes a walk of around three miles (5km).

Otherwise, continue (leaving Hotbank beyond a dyke to the left) along the wall for a further mile (1.5km) to the great ruined fort at Housesteads (fee on entry).

Continue along the right-hand side of the wall for a further half a mile (1km) beyond Housesteads, until a stile appears to the left – just after the wall has dropped down from the steep summit of King's Hill. Looking westwards from the stile, the wall runs along a series of crags to the left, there is a marshy hollow beneath the crags, and, to the right, a ridge runs parallel to the wall. Follow the indistinct route along this ridge, across a dyke and on to join the route of the Pennine Way, which cuts left to return to the wall.

Return to Steel Rigg along the original route.

22 Hexham

Length: 3¹/₂ miles (5.5km)
Height climbed: 250ft (80m) undulating
Grade: C
Public conveniences: Hexham
Public transport: Numerous bus and rail services
to Hexham

*Rough paths and clear tracks leading through
fine mixed woodland.*

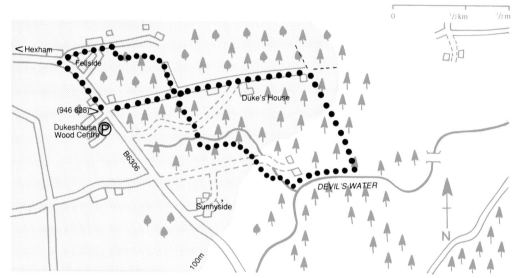

Follow the B6306 (to Blanchland) to a crest just
beyond Hexham. Park to the right of the road, near
the entrance to Dukeshouse Wood Centre. Walk
back down the road for about 400 yds (1/3 km).
Turn right down the road signposted for Fellside.

Turn right off the road at the signpost for the
footpath to Duke's House, into an area of mixed
woodland. There are a number of paths through the
wood, and it is important to stick to the main one.
This leads up a slope, bearing left along a flatter
section, then cutting hard right and running straight
up (with a field to the left) to a junction with
another track.

Walk straight across the track and through a
gap in the fence opposite, then bear half left along a
well-trodden path. After a short distance, another
track cuts across ahead; walk straight across this
and continue beyond. The path splits when it

reaches a fence – walk left, along the line of the
fence, and follow it down to the corner of a field;
then cut left, then right, into a wood of pine trees.

The path soon splits once more. Take the right-
hand path down the edge of the wood. When a
broad gully appears ahead, keep above and to the
left of it, on a path which gradually bears away by
the edge of an oak wood above the river.

This path shortly crosses another, smaller gully.
Bear slightly to the left across this, through a gap in
a crumbling dyke, and continue on the track
beyond. A track soon cuts off to the left. Ignore
this and carry straight on.

Continue until a T-junction is reached, then cut
left and follow a clear track up to a further, four-
way junction. Turn left and follow a clear track
past the Duke's House and back to the B6306.

23 Wylam

Length: 4^1/$_2$ miles (7km)
Height climbed: None
Grade: C
Public conveniences: Wylam
Public transport: Bus service from Newcastle

A short, flat riverside circuit on clear tracks.
Paths rough in places.

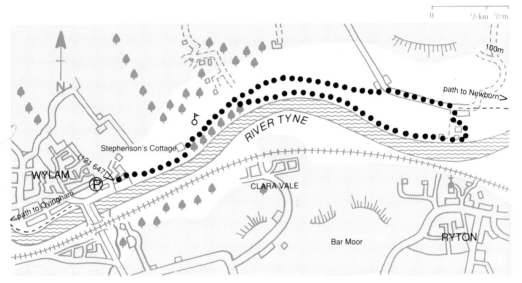

The little town of Wylam holds an unrivalled position in the history of the railways. The line between Wylam Colliery and the port of Lemington – five miles (8km) down the Tyne – carried the early steam locomotive *Puffing Billy*, built in 1813 by the pioneer William Hedley; while, by coincidence, the greatest name in the early history of rail, George Stephenson – the designer of *The Rocket* – was born in a little cottage by the side of the line. This path follows the route of the old line, and passes Stephenson's birthplace.

To reach Wylam, drive westwards out of Newcastle on the A69 and turn left when indicated. Drive through the town, down towards the river, and park in the car park (once Wylam Station) to the left of the road.

The path used for this route is part of a longer walkway, running from Newburn – three miles

(5km) to the east – to Ovingham – three miles (5km) up river to the west. For this walk, set off along the track signposted to Newburn.

After half a mile (1km), the track passes Stephenson's Cottage, which is now owned by the National Trust and open to the public for restricted periods (check with tourist offices for details). The track then continues between a golf course to the left and the tree-lined river to the right.

Gradually, the track pulls away from the riverside, and, after a mile (1.5km), reaches a row of cottages. A mile (1.5km) further on down the track is the town of Newburn but, for this route, turn right at the cottages. This track leads down to another terrace. Cut to the left, behind the terrace, then continue down to the river. Turn right along a rough path by the side of the Tyne – tidal as far up river as Wylam – to rejoin the original track.

24 Chopwell Wood

Length: ³/4-3 miles (1-5km)
Height climbed: Undulating
Grade: C
Public conveniences: None
Public transport: Bus service to Highfield – one mile (1.5km) from start of walks – from Newcastle

Three signposted forest walks on good tracks.

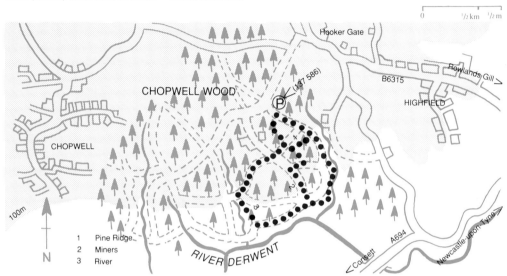

Chopwell wood is a fine, mixed forestry wood on the northern slopes above the River Derwent. The existence of the wood is recorded as early as the 12th century, when it was a part of the estates belonging to the Bishops of Durham. It is now in the ownership of the Forestry Commission but is a somewhat more interesting place than many other commercial woods, having a large number of broad-leaved trees interspersed amongst the conifers. This allows more air and light into the forest and encourages the undergrowth.

To reach Chopwell, drive south-west from Newcastle on the A694 Consett road. At Rowlands Gill *(25)* – four miles (6.5km) beyond the bridge across the Tyne between Newcastle and Blaydon – turn right on the B6315 road to Ryton. One and a

half miles (2.5km) from the junction, at Hooker Gate, turn left down a minor road leading to a car park in the forest.

There are three walks – the 'Pine Ridge', 'Miners', and 'River' walks in ascending order of length – colour-coded and well signposted. The two longer routes lead to a point giving a fine view over the wooded valley of the River Derwent, and the River Walk continues along the top of the valley for a while, passing above a fine oak wood covering the slope down to the river. The trees in this part of the wood were planted after the Napoleonic Wars of the early 19th century, to replace those which had been taken to build ships for the English fleet.

25 Derwent Walk

Length: Up to 5 miles (8km) or more (one way)
Height climbed: Negligible
Grade: A/B/C
Public conveniences: None
Public transport: Bus service from Newcastle to
Rowlands Gill and Consett (along A694)

*A lineal walk along a section of a longer
footpath, following the route of a disused
railway line.*

Rowlands Gill is a sprawling residential town in the
valley of the River Derwent. To reach it, drive
south-west from Newcastle on the A694 road to
Consett – Rowlands Gill is four miles (6.5km)
beyond the bridge over the Tyne at Blaydon. To
the east of the town (access off the B6314 road to
Burnopfield) is the National Trust property of
Gibside Chapel, the Palladian mausoleum of the
Bowes family, which was completed in 1812 and is
surrounded by parkland designed by Capability
Brown.

The town is on the route of the Derwent Walk
Country Park: a 10 mile (16km) long footpath
between Whickham (near Blaydon) and Consett to
the south-west, which follows the course of the old
railway line along the valley of the Derwent. This
particular route uses only a section of the path but,
obviously, it can be joined at any point and

followed for as far as is wished.

From the centre of Rowlands Gill, turn down
Stirlings Lane to a car park. Follow the path from
the car park leading up on to the old line and then
cut left, on to a bridge crossing high above the
river. From this point there are fine views of the
tree-lined river and the adjacent farmland. The
little ruin of 12th-century Friarside Chapel is
visible on the haugh to the west, three fields distant.

Follow the line as far as is wished. For this
route, walk as far as the village of Hamsterley, then
cut down to the road and pick up one of the
numerous buses along the A694 back to the start.
The line passes through a pleasant countryside of
hedge-lined fields and areas of broad-leaved and
conifer woodland. These woods are quite dense
and can restrict the view, particularly during the
summer.

26 Blanchland

Length: 3½ miles (5.5km)
Height climbed: 350ft (110m)
Grade: B
Public conveniences: Blanchland
Public transport: Blanchland is a stop on the bus
route between Consett and Townfield

*A short circuit through farmland, open
moorland and riverside woodland on rough
tracks and metalled roads.*

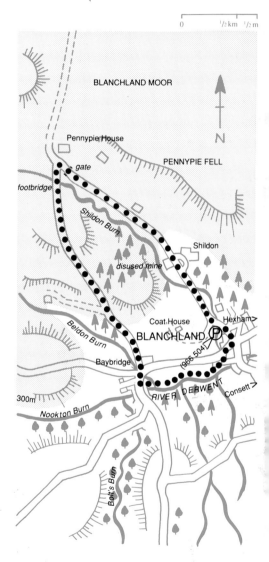

The village of Blanchland, though only small, is
one of the finest in Northumbria, and its pastoral
elegance comes as something of a surprise amidst
the bleak moors and hills of the area. The greater
part of the settlement was built in the 18th century,
on the site of a 12th-century abbey; but the great
gate-house on one side of the square is older: it
dates from the 15th century.

To reach the village, drive 10 miles (16km)
west of Consett on the B6278/B6306. Park in the
car park on the northern edge of the village and
start walking up the metalled road beside the
Shildon Burn; through woodland at first, but later
through open farmland. At one point, opposite
Shildon, there is the ruin of an old lead mine on
private land on the left-hand side of the road. The
village of Blanchland was originally built to house
lead miners.

Follow the road up to Pennypie. When a track
cuts right, up to the house, carry straight on through
a gate. Then turn left across a footbridge over the
burn and on along a clear track through heather
moorland. Watch for red grouse and curlew along
this stretch.

Follow the track until it joins a metalled road,
then cut left down to the road. Looking across the
valley, it is possible to see the chimneys of the old
lead mines on the moors over towards Weardale.

Turn right along the road until, just before it
crosses the River Derwent, a footpath cuts off to
the left, signposted for Blanchland. Follow the
path along the riverside, through a narrow band of
mixed woodland, back to the village.

27 Maiden Way

Length: 6 miles (9.5km)
Height climbed: 250ft (80m)
Grade: B
Public conveniences: None
Public transport: On bus route between Haltwhistle and Alston

Low-level walk along a disused railway line in a wooded valley; returning on Roman road through open moorland.

This walk starts at Lambley, a tiny village in the valley of the River South Tyne, nine miles (14.5km) north of the pleasant town of Alston on the A689 road to Brampton.

Turn down towards the river from the main street, along a footpath signposted for the Lambley Viaduct. The path cuts right, on the old railway line along the edge of the village, then cuts hard left (to avoid Station House), down a wooded slope. It passes under the arches of the disused rail viaduct and then climbs up again to rejoin the old railway.

Carry on along the line, which soon crosses the road leading into Waughold Holme. There appear to be two possible tracks starting on the far side of this track: take the right-hand one.

The route is now clear for a little over two miles (3km); generally passing through broad-leaved or conifer woodland, but with the trees occasionally thinning to allow a view of the steep wooded slope and occasional farms on the far side of the valley.

Shortly before the track reaches the old bridge over the A689 it runs very close to the road. Drop down to the road and continue until, just before the bridge, a driveway opens up to the right leading to Burnstones.

Turn into the drive and walk up to the right-hand side of Burnstones, from where a clear track cuts up the slope. The route is now signposted as part of the Pennine Way which, across this moorland section, follows the route of a Roman road known as the Maiden Way.

At one point the track approaches the road, to cross the Glendue Burn on a footbridge, before climbing onto the moors once again.

When the Pennine Way finally cuts off to the left, carry straight on down to join the A689, then cut right, along the road, to return to Lambley.

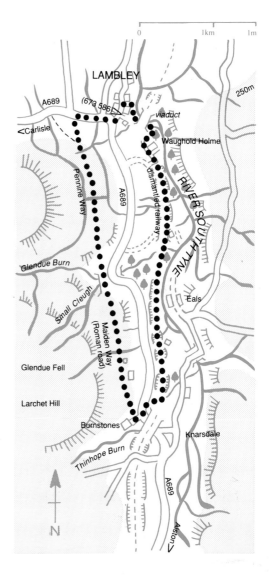

28 Allen Dale

Length: 7 miles (11km)
Height climbed: Negligible
Grade: B
Public conveniences: Allendale Town
Public transport: Bus service from Hexham

A sequence of footpaths, fields and quiet public roads, providing a circuit through the woodland and farmland of a quiet, rural valley.

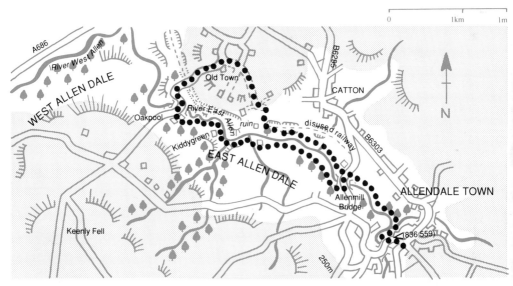

Allendale Town is a pleasant old former lead-mining town in East Allen Dale, ten miles (16km) south-west of Hexham along the B6305/B6304.

Start this walk from the Market Place, and leave the town on the road signposted to Whitfield. As the road winds down towards the river, a footpath cuts off to the right, signposted to Allenmill. Follow this path for three quarters of a mile (1.2km), through woodland and farmland by the riverside, to the Allenmill Bridge. Walk straight across the road and continue along the river bank beyond.

After half a mile (1km) the path splits, just before crossing a tiny burn. The main track leads up from the river towards Catton, but for this walk continue along the river bank.

After a further half a mile (1km) the path enters a wood. Watch for the faint path which leads up, at an angle, through the wood to a stile into a field.

Once in the field turn hard left towards a stile over a dyke; cross the dyke and walk diagonally across the field to a small ruin. Go through a gate beside the ruin onto a disused railway line. Cross this and go through another gate, almost directly opposite, into another field. At the top right-hand corner of this field is a stile. Cross this to join a track curving up to join a metalled road. Once on the road, ignore the first junction and continue to the second, where the metalled road cuts up to a house to the right, and a grass track carries straight on, between two dykes. Follow this track to Old Town, then cut left down a narrow road which drops steeply down to a picturesque bridge over the river.

Cross the bridge and turn left immediately, past Oakpool. Continue along the riverside path, through open grazing land and woodland on the valley flood plain, back to Allenmill Bridge.

Walk 28

29 Allenheads

Length: 5 miles (8km)
Height climbed: 600ft (180m)
Grade: B
Public conveniences: Allenheads
Public transport: Bus service from Hexham

Minor roads and footpaths forming a circuit through the moorland and hill-farmland around an old lead-mining settlement.

Allenheads sits at the very head of beautiful East Allen Dale; 1300ft (400m) above sea level. It is a tiny village, originally built to house people working in the lead mines of the area. There is a Heritage Centre in the village explaining its history, while the surrounding moorland is littered with the surviving traces of the industry.

Start from the centre of the village and head off up Rookhope Road. Follow this road as it climbs steeply for about three quarters of a mile (1.2km). A short distance after a cattle grid a clear track cuts off the road to the left. This leads past a quarry which once provided stone roof slates (an attractive feature of many of the buildings along this walk) up to the stone curricks on Dodd End. Cut right from the curricks, and continue with a dyke to the left.

When the dyke cuts left, near a large ruin, follow it, traversing the side of the hill behind a string of fine ruins. There are fine views to the old mine workings across the dale.

Behind Byerhope Farm the path becomes indistinct. Continue in the same direction until another track appears ahead. Cut half-right along this until it joins another track at a cairn. Follow this track for a short distance, up onto a ridge, watching out for a blue arrow marking the start of the bridleway back down to the road. Follow the blue-tipped posts which mark the route and then cross the road at the bottom and walk down the minor road opposite as it zig-zags down to the river.

Cross the river and follow the road to the left. When it breaks to the right, continue along the riverside footpath. This eventually joins the road once again. Cut left, across the river, then right, to return to Allenheads.

30 Westgate

Length: 3 miles (5km)
Height climbed: 450ft (140m)
Grade: B
Public conveniences: None
Public transport: Bus services along Weardale from Bishop Auckland stop at Westgate

A short circuit in a hill valley, through woodland and grazing land, and passing ruins of the lead-mining industry. Path rough in places.

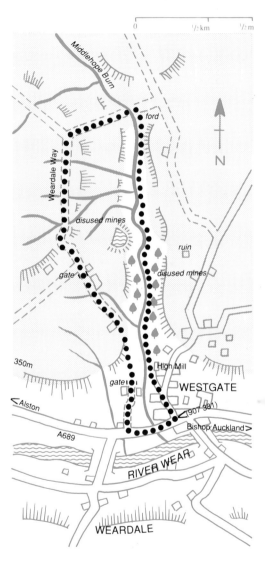

Westgate is a small village in Weardale. Originally it was the site of a hunting lodge of the Bishops of Durham (at the 'west gate' to the deer park), but in more recent centuries it became a centre for the lead-mining industry. The Weardale Way – a 78 mile (125km) footpath from the mouth of the river to Cowshill – passes through the village, and this walk follows a section of its route.

To reach the village, drive 25 miles (40km) north-west from Bishop Auckland on the A689 Alston road. Park in the main street and start walking up a small, unsignposted road heading northwards. A short way up this road, cut left at the sign for a public footpath and continue up to High Mill. Go through the gate and pass to the left of this private house, then continue up a fine wooded glen.

Continue along the burnside path, passing a great many ruined relics of the lead-mining days along the way, clustered on the narrow flood-plain of the burn. **Please approach all old workings with care.**

After a little over a mile (1.5km), the valley – now running through open grazing land, and with moorland on the slopes ahead – starts to bend to the west, and suddenly to narrow. At this point a rough track comes in from the right and crosses the Middlehope Burn by a rough ford. Cross at this point and continue on the track beyond, leading up between two dykes to a junction. Turn left at the junction and stay with the track until it cuts hard right. At this point carry straight on, through a gate, and along a rough track down the side of the field beyond.

Follow this track past two buildings, then carry straight on across the middle of a field to a gate. Go through this and continue with a dyke to the right-hand side, leading down to a farm. Go through the farm and down the drive beyond to the road. Turn left to return to Westgate.

31 Wolsingham

Length: 8¹/₂ miles (13.5km)
Height climbed: 800ft (240m)
Grade: A
Public conveniences: Wolsingham
Public transport: Bus service to Wolsingham and Frosterley from Bishop Auckland

A long circuit on a riverside footpath through farmland and woodland, a track over open moorland, and quiet public roads. Fine views.

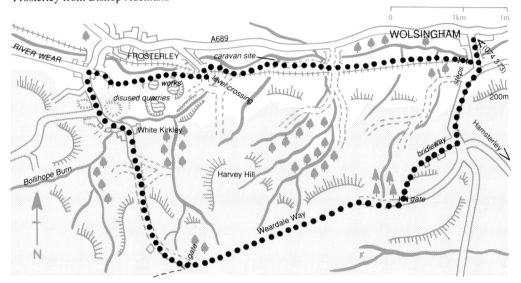

To reach the little industrial town of Wolsingham, in Weardale, drive some 12 miles (19.5km) west of Bishop Auckland on the A689. Park in the town centre and walk south on the minor road to Hamsterley.

After a climb of one mile (1.5km), cut right along a farm track signposted as a bridleway. At the track's western end, it passes through two gates and then disappears. When it does so, cut half left, aiming for the top of a plantation which appears ahead.

Opposite the corner of the wood, there is a gate in a dyke. Go through this and then cut right, along a clear track to the left of the dyke. This fine stretch of open moorland continues for about two miles (3km) until, shortly after passing to the left of a stand of beech trees, a gate appears in the dyke to the right. Go through this and follow the clear track beyond down to the little hamlet of White

Kirkley, and on towards the town of Frosterley beyond.

Cut right before the river and head east along a waymarked track, through a farmyard and on to a large mineral works. Beyond the works cut left, over a level crossing, then right, through a gate, and on along a rough path across the flat grazing land by the river, with the railway line to the right.

Shortly after crossing the Bollihope Burn, the path reaches a caravan site. Follow the path between the site and the river until a metalled road appears up to the right. Carry on along this road for about half a mile (1km) until it cuts left over a bridge across the river. At this point, carry straight on along a narrow footpath by the railway line. This path continues for a further mile (1.5km) before climbing a flight of steps onto the bridge carrying the road from Wolsingham on which the route began. Turn left to return to the town.

32 Bearpark

Length: 4¹/₂ miles (7km)
Height climbed: Undulating
Grade: B
Public conveniences: Durham
Public transport: Bus services from Durham
centre to Nevilles Cross

*A circuit on good pathways through mixed
farming, housing and industrial landscape.*

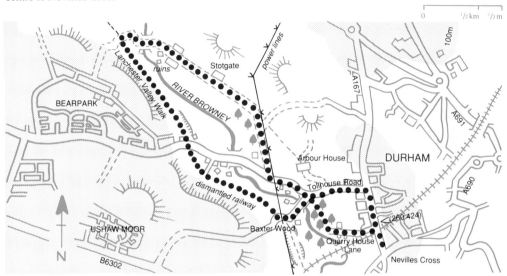

On the western outskirts of the cathedral city of
Durham is Nevilles Cross; the site of a battle in
1346 between David II of Scotland and an army of
northern English lords. The English were
victorious, and the Scottish king was imprisoned in
London for 11 years.

Park in Nevilles Cross and start walking down
Quarry House Lane – just to the north of the
railway line. Follow this road until the sign
indicates 'farm road only'; then cut left down a
footpath along a wooded slope.

After a short distance, there is a gate leading
into a field. Go through this and walk along the
right-hand side of the field. When the field ends
the path recommences, running along the side of
the River Browney. When a bridge over the river
is reached, turn left across it and follow the road
beyond up to a farm. A short distance after the
farm, the track is crossed by a disused railway line.

Turn right along this. After three quarters of a mile
(1km) the track crosses a minor road and then
continues beyond it. This section of line (between
Durham and Lanchester) is now designated the
'Lanchester Valley Walk'.

Continue along the track, under the shadow of a
hill on which are perched the terraces of the mining
village of Bearpark. After a further three quarters
of a mile (1km), the track is crossed by another
track. The Lanchester Valley path continues
straight ahead, but for this route, cut right; down
across the Browney, past the slight ruins of the old
Bishops' residence of Beau Repaire on a mound by
the river, and on. A good track leads past two
farms before dropping down to the road between
Bearpark (a corruption of 'Beau Repaire') and
Durham. Turn left along the road (Tollhouse
Road), which soon runs into housing as it returns to
Nevilles Cross.

33 Cow Green Reservoir

Length: 7¹/₂ miles (12km)
Height climbed: 400ft (120m)
Grade: A
Public conveniences: Car park
Pubic transport: Bus service to Forest-in-Teesdale
– two miles (3km) from walk – from Barnard Castle

*A clear circuit along footpaths and quiet
public roads; passing moorland, rocky crags
and a shallow, upland river, plus a fine
waterfall.*

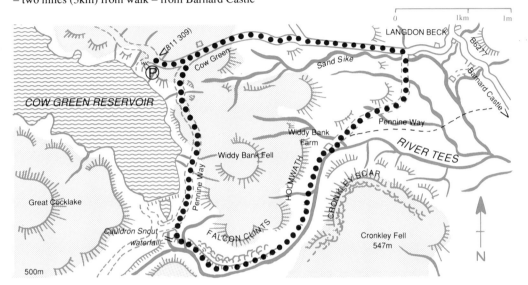

Cow Green Reservoir was formed in 1970, by
damming the waters of the Tees near the river's
source under Cross Fell – the highest peak in the
Pennines. To reach the reservoir, drive north-west
from Barnard Castle on the B6277 road to Alston.
Seven miles (11km) after Middleton-in-Teesdale,
the road reaches the hamlet of Langdon Beck.
Turn left, down a minor road leading to a car park
by the reservoir, where there are information
boards describing the wildlife to be found in the
area.

Start walking back down the road. After a
short distance, a road cuts off to the right. One and
a half miles (2.5km) down that road is the Cauldron
Snout waterfall; but for this route, ignore the
junction and continue across the heather moorland
on the original road.

After one mile (1.5km) there is a junction.
Carry straight on. After a further mile (1.5km) a
track cuts off to the right signposted for Cauldron
Snout. Follow this winding track over the
moorland, with the dramatic cliffs of Cronkley Scar
above the River Tees ahead. The track ends at
Widdy Bank Farm, and the walk (now following
the route of the Pennine Way) continues on a rough
footpath through the stony meadows of the
Holmwath. When Cronkley Scar ends on the far
side of the river, however, the basalt cliffs of
Falcon Clints take over on the near side. The
meadows end and the path is forced to cross areas
of boulders and scree above the water's edge, as the
river winds up to Cauldron Snout.

This is much the best approach to the falls: a
thundering 200ft/60m fall in a series of steep
cascades. Climb up the rocky slope beside the falls
and then continue along the metalled road beyond;
leading up to the road, a short distance to the east
of the car park.

34 High Force

Length: 7¹/₂ miles (12km)
Height climbed: 450ft (140m)
Grade: A
Public conveniences: Bowlees Visitor Centre
Public transport: Bus service from Barnard Castle to Bowlees

A series of rough paths through open moorland and juniper scrub; running by a river for much of the way and passing a notable waterfall.

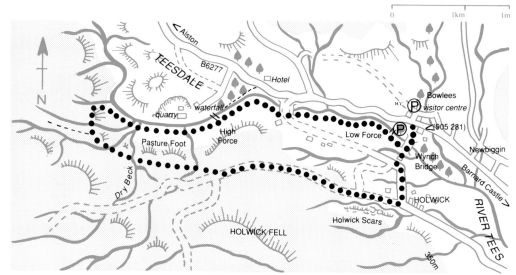

High Force drops the River Tees 70ft (20m) into a large pool surrounded by vertical cliffs. It is the most dramatic natural feature in the area, and access to it is relatively easy – either along the short path from the High Force Hotel, or by the longer track described below.

To reach the start of the walk, drive 12 miles (19km) north-west of Barnard Castle on the B6277 Alston road. Park either at the Bowlees Visitor Centre (signposted from the road) or in one of the roadside parking spaces beyond.

Start walking down the footpath which starts opposite the western entrance to Bowlees; signposted to Wynch Bridge. Walk through the fields down to the wooded river-bank, cross the narrow bridge and turn right along the river.

Follow the river for two miles (3km) to High Force, then continue along the well-trodden path

beyond; watching out for the warning red flag which indicates blasting at the quarry across the river. Just under a mile (1.5km) beyond the quarry the river makes a right-angled turn to the right. On the apex of this bend the river is joined by a boggy rill, which cuts across the path. Just before the rill there is a fence with a gate in it. Turn left before the fence and walk along it to a gate in a dyke at the top of the field. Go through this, walk up to the grassy track running across the way ahead and cut left to climb on to the heathery shoulder of Holwick Fell. After about a mile (1.5km), a fence crosses the track, crossed by a stile. Walk across the moor beyond to join a good track which comes down from the hill to the right. Bear left and follow it down to join the public road at Holwick. Cut left down the road and, when it turns left, carry straight on along the footpath to Wynch Bridge.

Walk 34

35 Cotherstone

Length: 6 miles (9.5km)
Height climbed: 250ft (80m)
Grade: B
Public conveniences: None
Public transport: Bus service from Barnard
Castle

*A circuit along rough paths and quiet roads,
and through open farmland and woodland,
above a narrow, wooded valley.*

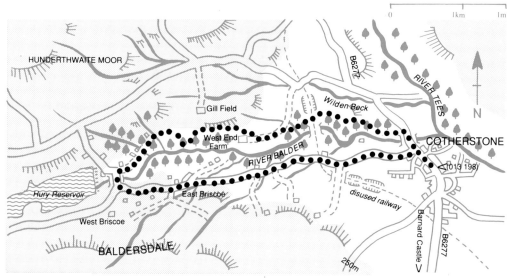

Cotherstone is a quiet village in Teesdale, three and
a half miles (5.5km) north-west of Barnard Castle
on the B6277. Park in the village centre and walk
northwards, crossing the narrow road bridge over
the River Balder and then turning left, at the sign
for a footpath, into a field.

Cut half right across the field towards a low,
wooded slope. Climb this on a rough path, cross a
stile into a field at the top of the slope and then turn
left, keeping the fence to the left.

Continue on this course – with the steep, tree-
lined valley down to the left – through a number of
fields, until the old railway line is reached. Cross
the line using two stiles, then continue until a track
crosses the route. Cut left along this track and
follow it to West End Farm.

Cut right at the farm, through a gate into a
field; then left, along the dyke. Exit by the second
gate on the left and then continue along the edge of
the wood through farmland.

At one point, the path cuts down into the woods
to the left before quickly climbing into the
farmland again. At this point, cut diagonally right
across a field to a gate and then continue towards
an old building with a gate beside it. Cross the stile
by the gate and then cut half left, down to the dyke
along the bottom of the field. Follow the dyke into
the woods and cross a small footbridge over a tiny
burn.

Carry on beyond the bridge, with the dyke to
the right, towards another old stone building. Go
through the gate by this building and then follow
the track beyond as it curves to the left, in front of a
stone cottage, and then continues across a field to
join the road.

Turn left along the road, then left again at the
next junction, to return to Cotherstone.

Walk 35

36 Barnard Castle

Length: 4 miles (6.5km).
Height climbed: Negligible
Grade: B
Public conveniences: Barnard Castle
Public transport: Numerous bus services to
Barnard Castle

*A walk through riverside woodland and open
farmland on tracks of varying quality. Castle
ruins and pleasant countryside.*

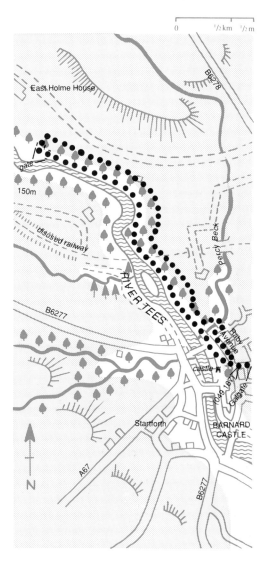

Park in the Galgate (roads from the north and east
enter the town along this wide main street) and
walk down to the end of the street. At the point
where the main street makes a right-angled turn
into Horsemarket, there is a church. Walk down
the right-hand side of this building. Behind the
church there is a grassy space, on the far side of
which are the ruins of 12th-century Barnard Castle
(pay a small fee on entry).

Near the end of the church is a signpost
indicating the direction for a number of local
walks. For this route (shown on the signpost as
'Walk 1'), cut right along a tarmac road which
gradually drops down to the bank of the River
Tees. After a short distance a bridge cuts left,
across the river. Ignore this and take the path
which crosses the footbridge over the little Percy
Beck and then continues by the riverside.

Follow this path through mixed woodland, past
the twin supports of a dismantled rail bridge, and
then on, for a further mile (1.5km) or so, through a
pleasant rocky gorge to a small meadow by the
riverside. Go through a gate into this meadow and
follow the dyke to the right for about 100 yards
(90m). When a gate appears to the right, go
through it, then climb the wooded slope beyond to
a fence by a field. Cross the fence and turn right.

There is no path, but the way is clear. Continue
through a succession of fields, keeping the
woodland across the fence to the right. The route
crosses the old railway line and then continues,
providing fine views of Barnard Castle and the
surrounding farmland, before cutting into the
woods, turning to the left and dropping to join a
track through the woods around Percy Beck. Cut
left along this track, then right, over a bridge across
the beck, and climb the steps beyond to reach Raby
Avenue, leading down to the town centre.

37 Eggleston Abbey

Length: 3 miles (5km)
Height climbed: Negligible
Grade: C
Public conveniences: Barnard Castle
Public transport: Numerous bus services to
Barnard Castle

*A flat, low-level walk through fields and along
a quiet public road. Pleasant river scenery
plus a ruined abbey.*

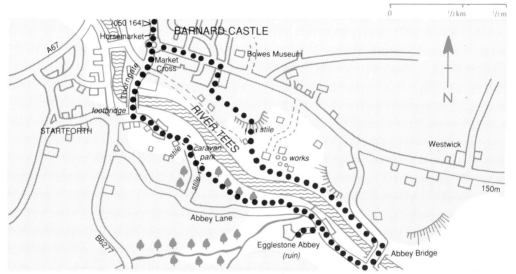

Barnard Castle is a fine old market town situated at
the eastern end of Teesdale. Its main features are
the splendid Bowes Museum and Art Gallery, and
the ruin of its 12th-century castle, perched above
the old bridge over the River Tees at the western
end of the town *(36)*.

Start this walk from the Galgate – the broad
street in the centre of the town. Walk down to the
end of the street nearest the castle and then turn
left, down the Horsemarket. Carry straight on
beyond the Market Cross (which acts as a
roundabout), down the Thorngate and across the
footbridge beyond.

Climb the slope on the far side of the river and
turn left along a road. When the road ends carry on
to join the tarmac road running through the caravan
park ahead. Bear right along this, then cut left
across a stile into a field, just before a line of trees

starts along the roadside. Walk along the left-hand
edge of the field, and then continue across the three
fields beyond to reach a tarmac road. Cut left
along the road, passing the picturesque ruins of the
12th-century Egglestone Abbey (entry free).

Continue along the road for a quarter of a mile
(0.5km) and then cut left, across the small road
bridge over the river. Once over the bridge cut left,
off the road, onto a rough path which leads through
dense woodland down to the riverside, where the
trees give way on the right to open grazing land.

Once the riverside path has passed the high
fencing around the sewage works, cut half right
across a field towards a small stone building. Just
before reaching this building cut right, up the hill,
towards a stile. Cross the stile, and another soon
after, then turn left and follow a broad track
between two fences back to Barnard Castle.

38 Bowes

Length: 7^1/$_2$ miles (12km)
Height climbed: 300ft (90m)
Grade: A
Public conveniences: None
Public transport: Bus services from Barnard
Castle, Darlington and Newcastle

*A long walk on public roads, rough tracks and
open moorland. Some navigation required.*

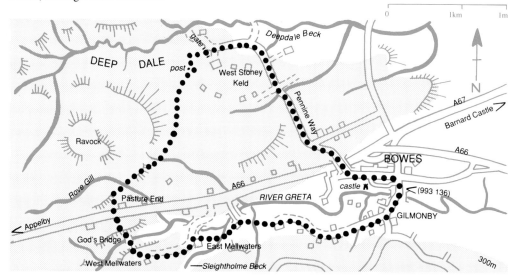

Bowes is a small cluster of houses surrounded by
the moors of the eastern Pennines, four miles
(6.5km) south-west of Barnard Castle on the A67.
The village is situated on the site of a Roman fort,
built to command Stainmore Pass to the west. In
the 12th century a keep was built in a corner of the
fort, and the impressive ruin of this stronghold still
dominates the village.

Walk to the western end of the village and
follow the minor road which cuts right, across a
bridge over the A66, and on up the hill beyond.

Keep to the right past the gate into West Stoney
Keld Farm, then go through a gate and cut hard left
to follow the line of a dyke. Follow the dyke until
it cuts left. From the corner a post is visible on the
horizon, half left ahead. Head for the post, then
continue beyond, across open moorland, skirting
around to the left of the low hill of Ravock. There

is no clear path, but the route is marked by
occasional yellow marks. By the time the 'path'
has crossed Rove Gill it should have joined a dyke
to the left-hand side. Follow this dyke until it
reaches the A66 at Pasture End.

Cross the road (generally busy) and continue on
the track directly opposite: dropping down to cross
the River Greta on God's Bridge – a striking
natural limestone structure.

Beyond the bridge, cut half-left through a gate
and then continue across the field beyond to West
Mellwaters. Walk past the front of this building
and then continue across two fields to join the track
to East Mellwaters. Go through the gate beyond
the farm and carry on to the footbridge over the
Sleightholme Beck; then on, past three more farms,
to Gilmonby. Turn left along a minor road to
return to Bowes.

39 Roseberry Topping

Length: 2 miles (3km) with possible extensions
Height climbed: 750ft (230m)
Grade: B/C
Public conveniences: Car park
Public transport: None

A short, steep climb to a rocky torr; plus possible extensions, including a short circuit. Fine views and clear paths.

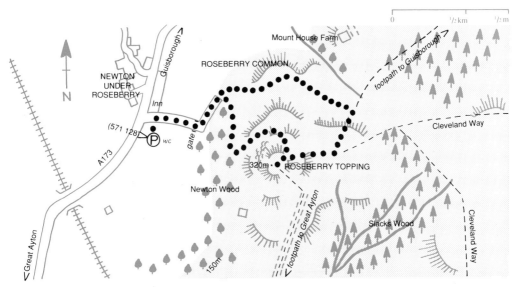

To the south of Cleveland, beyond the flat farmland and cluttered townscape around the lower waters of the River Tees, the Cleveland Hills rise to a series of modest summits. The most prominent of these, though not the highest, is the conical Roseberry Topping, with its distinctive rocky peak.

To reach the hill, drive to the southern edge of Middlesbrough and cut east on the A171 to Guisborough, then double back to the south on the A173 to Stokesley. After three miles (5km) the road reaches the tiny village of Newton under Roseberry. Drive to the far end of the village and turn left into the car park, a little beyond the inn.

Walk back to the end of the car park nearest the village and turn right up a clear track between hedges, with fields beyond on either side. This track leads straight up to the edge of an oak wood which fringes the foot of the hill. Go through a

gate into the wood. There are a number of paths through the trees ahead. For the easiest route turn hard left, then, after a short distance, double back to the right onto a good track which starts to climb the hill at a slant. The path to the summit is never in doubt.

From the peak there are many options. The map illustrates a possible loop to the north, but a number of other footpaths are clearly visible from the rocky summit, leading north-east to Guisborough and south-west to Great Ayton. In addition, the hill is crossed by the Cleveland Way, a long-distance footpath around the North York Moors. The Way passes Captain Cook's monument (he was born at Marton, now on the southern outskirts of Middlesbrough) which is visible on a hill to the south-east.

40 Boulby

Length: 2-4 miles (3-6.5km)
Height climbed: 350ft (110m)
Grade: B
Public conveniences: None
Public transport: None

Fine views, but not for the faint-hearted or for vertigo sufferers. A cliff-top walk, passing disused quarries. Return by quiet roads.

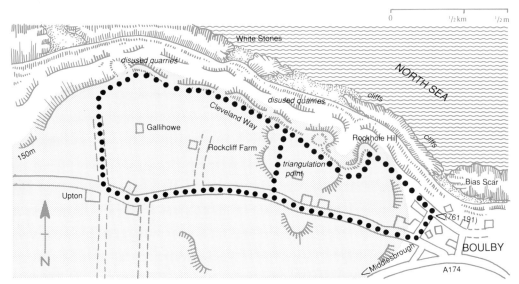

Boulby is a tiny coastal village near the southern border of Cleveland, on the edge of the industrial area around the mouth of the River Tees. To reach it, drive about 22 miles (35km) east of Middlesbrough along the A174, passing through the grand Victorian coastal resort of Saltburn-by-the-Sea.

Turn left into Boulby. Parking is limited but it should be possible to find a space.

The area is dominated by the chimneys of the huge Boulby Potash Mine, the shafts and galleries of which reach out far under the North Sea.

Turn left in front of a row of cottages at the western edge of the village, which sit near the edge of the 350ft (100m) cliffs – the cliffs reach a height of 600ft (180m) further to the north. A path starts beyond the cottages, along the cliff edge. This path is a section of the Cleveland Way: a long-distance footpath 112 miles (180km) in length; leading north, from Filey in Yorkshire up the coast to Saltburn, then south, to Helmsley in the Yorkshire Moors.

Follow the path along the cliffs until it cuts left, behind the bracken covered Rockhole Hill, before rejoining the cliffs beyond. North of Rockhole Hill, the cliffs are heavily indented by the massive labours of the alum quarriers in past centuries.

After a short distance, a footpath leads off to the left, past a triangulation pillar and on to the road. Cut left to complete the shortened version of this route.

Otherwise, continue beside the quarries – passing an information board explaining the manner and purpose of the alum industry – then take the next footpath leading down to the left to Upton. Once the road is reached, turn left, back towards Boulby.

Walk 40

BARTHOLOMEW WALKS SERIES (Contd)

WALK OBAN, MULL & LOCHABER
0 7028 0801 6 £3·95

WALK THE PEAK DISTRICT
0 7028 0710 9 £4·99

MORE WALKS IN THE PEAK DISTRICT
0 7028 0951 9 £4·95

WALK PERTHSHIRE
0 7028 0766 4 £3·95

WALK LOCH NESS & THE RIVER SPEY
0 7028 0787 7 £3·95

**WALK ROYAL DEESIDE
& NORTH EAST SCOTLAND**
0 7028 0898 9 £3·95

WALK LOTHIAN, THE BORDERS & FIFE
0 7028 0803 2 £3·95

WALK SNOWDONIA & NORTH WALES
0 7028 0804 0 £3·95

WALK THE NEW FOREST
0 7028 0810 5 £4·99

WALK THE NORTH DOWNS
0 7028 0742 7 £4·99

WALK THE SOUTH DOWNS
0 7028 0811 3 £4·99

WALK THE NORTH YORK MOORS
0 7028 0743 5 £4·99

WALK THE SOUTH PENNINES
0 7028 0955 1 £4·95

WALK NORTHUMBRIA
0 7028 0959 4 £4·95

**WALK SOUTH WALES
& THE WYE VALLEY**
0 7028 0904 7 £3·95

NORTHUMBRIA WALKING PACK
Containing a copy of *Walk Northumbria* and a folded
copy of the Northumberland & Durham Leisure
Map in a clear, plastic carrying wallet.
0 7028 1216 1 £6·99

WALK SOUTH WEST SCOTLAND
0 7028 0900 4 £3·95

Guides in this series may be purchased from good bookshops. In the event of difficulty copies may be obtained by post.
Please send your order with your remittance to
**BARTHOLOMEW BOOKSERVICE BY POST,
PO BOX 29, DOUGLAS, ISLE OF MAN, BRITISH ISLES.**

NAME _____

ADDRESS _____

_____

Please enclose a cheque or postal order made out to 'Bartholomew' for the amount due and allow 25 pence per book
postage & packing fee up to a maximum of £3.00.
While every effort is made to keep prices low, it is sometimes necessary to increase cover prices at short notice.
Bartholomew reserves the right to show new retail prices on covers which may differ from those previously advertised in
the text or elsewhere.

BARTHOLOMEW WALKS SERIES

Designed to meet the requirements of both experienced and inexperienced walkers, the guides in this series are ideal for anyone who enjoys exploring on foot. They describe the best routes across our greatest walking country from Inverness to the New Forest and Cork & Kerry.

● In each guide, there are at least 30 carefully chosen, easy-to-follow walks over rights of way, with detailed route descriptions accompanying special maps.

● Country walks are graded according to distance and terrain and start from a convenient parking area. The route always returns to the car park, usually by a circular walk and, where appropriate, access by public transport is also possible.

● Notes on local history, geography and wildlife add interest to the walks and the unique notebook format is especially easy to use.

WALK CORK & KERRY

0 7028 0949 7 £4·95

WALK THE CORNISH COASTAL PATH

A special format step-by-step guide to the entire length of the Cornish Coastal Path (Marsland Mouth - Cremyll).

0 7028 0902 0 £4·99

WALK THE COTSWOLDS

0 7028 0908 X £4·99

WALK THE DALES

0 7028 0800 8 £4·99

MORE WALKS IN THE DALES

0 7028 0948 9 £4·95

YORKSHIRE DALES VISITOR'S PACK

Containing a copy of *Walk the Dales* and a folded 1 inch map of the Yorkshire Dales in a clear, plastic carrying wallet.

0 7028 0932 2 £6·99

WALK DARTMOOR

0 7028 0688 9 £3·95

WALK DEVON & CORNWALL

0 7028 1283 8 £4·99

WALK DORSET & HARDY'S WESSEX

0 7028 0906 3 £3·95

WALK EDINBURGH & THE PENTLANDS

0 7028 1280 3 £4·99

WALK EXMOOR & THE QUANTOCKS

0 7028 0910 1 £3·95

WALK HERTS & BUCKS

0 7028 0953 5 £4·95

WALK THE ISLE OF WIGHT

0 7028 1279 X £4·99

WALK THE LAKES

0 7028 8111 2 £4·99

MORE WALKS IN THE LAKES

0 7028 0819 9 £4·99

LAKE DISTRICT WALKING PACK

Containing a copy of *Walk the Lakes* and a folded 1 inch map of the Lake District in a clear, plastic carrying wallet.

0 7028 0876 8 £6·99

WALK LOCH LOMOND & THE TROSSACHS

0 7028 0744 3 £4·99